INSTRUCTION AND THE LEARNING ENVIRONMENT

James W. Keefe
John M. Jenkins

EYE ON EDUCATION
6 DEPOT WAY WEST, SUITE 106
LARCHMONT, NY 10538
(914) 833–0551
(914) 833–0761 fax

Library of Congress Cataloging-in-Publication Data

Keefe, James W.
    Instruction and the learning environment / James W. Keefe, John M.
Jenkins.
        p.   cm.
    Includes bibliographical references (p.).
    ISBN 1-883001-28-5
    1. School supervision--United States. 2. Learning. 3. Teaching-
-United States. 4. Educational leadership--United States.
I. Jenkins, John M. II. Title.
LB2806.4.K44 1997
371.2'01--dc20
                                                            96-32417
                                                               CIP

10 9 8 7 6 5 4 3 2

Editorial and production services provided by Richard H. Adin Freelance
Editorial Services, 9 Orchard Drive, Gardiner, NY 12525 (914-883-5884)

Published by Eye On Education:

Block Scheduling: A Catalyst for Change in High Schools
by Robert Lynn Canady and Michael D. Rettig

Teaching in the Block
edited by Robert Lynn Canady and Michael D. Rettig

Educational Technology: Best Practices from America's Schools
by William C. Bozeman and Donna J. Baumbach

The Educator's Brief Guide to Computers in the Schools
by Eugene F. Provenzo, Jr.

Handbook of Educational Terms and Applications
by Arthur K. Ellis and Jeffrey T. Fouts

Research on Educational Innovations
by Arthur K. Ellis and Jeffrey T. Fouts

Research on School Restructuring
by Arthur K. Ellis and Jeffrey T. Fouts

Hands-on Leadership Tools for Principals
by Ray Calabrese, Gary Short, and Sally Zepeda

The Principal as Steward
by Jack McCall

The Principal's Edge
by Jack McCall

Leadership: A Relevant and Practical Role for Principals
by Gary M. Crow, L. Joseph Matthews, and Lloyd E. McCleary

Organizational Oversight:
Planning and Scheduling for Effectiveness
by David A. Erlandson, Peggy L. Stark, and Sharon M. Ward

Motivating Others: Creating the Conditions
by David P. Thompson

Oral and Nonverbal Expression
by Ivan Muse

Instruction and the Learning Environment
by James W. Keefe and John M. Jenkins

Interpersonal Sensitivity
by John R. Hoyle and Harry M. Crenshaw

Directory of Innovations in Elementary Schools
by Jane McCarthy and Suzanne Still

The School Portfolio:
A Comprehensive Framework for School Improvement
by Victoria L. Bernhardt

The Administrator's Guide to School-Community Relations
by George E. Pawlas

Innovations in Parent and Family Involvement
by William Rioux and Nancy Berla

The Performance Assessment Handbook
Volume 1: Portfolios and Socratic Seminars
by Bil Johnson

The Performance Assessment Handbook
Volume 2: Performances and Exhibitions
by Bil Johnson

Bringing the NCTM Standards to Life
by Lisa B. Owen and Charles E. Lamb

Mathematics the Write Way
by Marilyn S. Neil

School-to-Work
by Arnold H. Packer and Marion W. Pines

Transforming Education Through Total Quality
Management: A Practitioner's Guide
by Franklin P. Schargel

Quality and Education: Critical Linkages
by Betty L. McCormick

The Educator's Guide to Implementing Outcomes
by William J. Smith

Schools for All Learners: Beyond the Bell Curve
by Renfro C. Manning

FOREWORD

The School Leadership Library was designed to show practicing and aspiring principals what they should know and be able to do to be effective leaders of their schools. The books in this series were written to answer the question, "How can we improve our schools by improving the effectiveness of our principals?"

Success in the principalship, like in other professions, requires mastery of a knowledge and skills base. One of the goals of the National Policy Board for Educational Administration (sponsored by NAESP, NASSP, AASA, ASCD, NCPEA, UCEA, and other professional organizations) was to define and organize that knowledge and skill base. The result of our efforts was the development of a set of 21 "domains," building blocks representing the core understandings and capabilities required of successful principals.

The 21 domains of knowledge and skills are organized under four broad areas: Functional, Programmatic, Interpersonal and Contextual. They are as follows:

FUNCTIONAL DOMAINS
Leadership
Information Collection
Problem Analysis
Judgment
Organizational Oversight
Implementation
Delegation

PROGRAMMATIC DOMAINS
Instruction and the Learning
Environment
Curriculum Design
Student Guidance and Development
Staff Development
Measurement and Evaluation
Resource Allocation

INTERPERSONAL DOMAINS
Motivating Others
Interpersonal Sensitivity
Oral and Nonverbal Expression
Written Expression

CONTEXTUAL DOMAINS
Philosophical and Cultural
Values
Legal and Regulatory Applications
Policy and Political Influences
Public Relations

These domains are not discrete, separate entities. Rather, they evolved only for the purpose of providing manageable descriptions of essential content and practice so as to better understand the entire complex role of the principalship. Because human behavior comes in "bunches" rather than neat packages, they are also overlapping pieces of a complex puzzle. Consider the domains as converging streams of behavior that spill over one another's banks but that all contribute to the total reservoir of knowledge and skills required of today's principals.

The School Leadership Library was established by General Editors David Erlandson and Al Wilson to provide a broad examination of the content and skills in all of the domains. The authors of each volume in this series offer concrete and realistic illustrations and examples, along with reflective exercises. You will find their work to be of exceptional merit, illustrating with insight the depth and interconnectedness of the domains. This series provides the fullest, most contemporary, and most useful information available for the preparation and professional development of principals.

Scott D. Thomson
Executive Secretary
National Policy Board for
Educational Administration

If you would like information about how to become a member of the **School Leadership Library**, please contact

Eye On Education
6 Depot Way West, Suite 106
Larchmont, NY 10538
(914) 883-0551
(914) 833-0761 FAX

ABOUT THE AUTHORS

James W. Keefe is the author of more than 50 books, articles, and assessment tools. Currently an educational consultant, he is the former Director of Research for the National Association of Secondary School Principals. He has taught at the junior high and the senior high levels and has served as a high school assistant principal and principal. He has also taught at the University of Southern California and Loyola Marymount University in Los Angeles.

Keefe has served on various national boards and committees, including the national panel for the U.S. Department of Education Center on Organization and Restructuring of Schools at the University of Wisconsin, Madison, and the advisory committee for the Coalition of Essential Schools.

John M. Jenkins has written some 30 articles and book chapters, and serves as the instruction department chair for the *International Journal of Educational Reform*. He was a high school principal for over four decades, and served as Director of the P.K. Yonge Development Research School on the campus of the University of Florida. He had previously taught at elementary, middle, and high schools. Jenkins currently teaches graduate level courses at the University of Florida and supervises graduate elementary school interns.

PREFACE

The American school has only one indigenous technology: instruction. Everything else that happens in and around the school—whether it be serving food in the cafeteria, methods for maintaining financial accountability, or the very buildings that house the school—is borrowed from another discipline and must be evaluated in terms of how well it facilitates the school's core technology, the teaching and learning process. Even the concept and practice of "leadership" has been developed primarily outside of the school. Leadership in the school only has meaning as it is used to enhance instruction. In a very real sense all the leadership that the principal displays should be instructional leadership.

This statement about instruction as the core technology of the school is more than a general platitude. It is a very direct statement, with very practical implications, for the principal who would display leadership in the school. Not only is the teaching-learning process the major focus of the school, it is the theme that gives central meaning to the professional value of teachers—by far the most numerous and most important of the adults who work under the principal's leadership. Teachers value themselves professionally primarily on the basis of their instructional expertise; it is difficult for them to be enthusiastic followers of a principal who does not have a reasonably high level of instructional expertise. There is no substitute for this principal attribute: the principal must thoroughly understand the teaching-learning process and must be able to articulate that understanding in communications with teachers, parents, students, and others.

Much is known about the instructional process, and many books have been written on it. In considering a single text for the principal on this fundamental school topic, it is truly a formidable task to determine what ought to be included and what ought to be excluded. James Keefe and John Jenkins have taken on this daunting task in this volume and have used their broad and diverse experience in public schools, universities, and professional associations to focus on a set of related topics that is both sufficient in breadth to eliminate gaps in understanding the instructional process, as it is promoted through school practice, and sufficient in depth to provide the principal with an integrated understanding that will encourage continued growth and development.

The principal or prospective principal who reads through this book and carefully considers its implications for instruction in the school will acquire a strong foundation for demonstrating instructional leadership. Such principal will recognize the need for conceptualizing the school as a learning organization and will learn how to analyze and construct the elements that support it. Keefe and Jenkins carefully build the reader's understanding of information processing, the instructional process, instructional models, learning styles, authentic pedagogy, and classroom environments. Using these building blocks they show how assessment, scheduling, and organization patterns may be analyzed and shaped to serve the purposes of instruction. They explore the crucial relationship between student motivation and learning. Finally, they conclude by providing the principal with a tool, in the form of action research, that can be effectively used for the continuation and systematic improvement of instruction.

This volume should prove to be one of the most valuable books on the principal's shelf throughout his or her career. It is the essence of what school is all about.

David A. Erlandson
Alfred P. Wilson

TABLE OF CONTENTS

INTRODUCTION

All institutions resist change, but education has been more cautious than most. The almost perverse tenacity that educational institutions have shown in clinging to traditional practices led leadership guru Peter Drucker in 1968 to comment that, "The first teacher ever, that priest in preliterate Mesopotamia who sat down outside the temple with the kids and began to draw figures with a twig in the sand, would be perfectly at home in most classrooms in the world today."

Many educators remember the provocative educational film of the 1960s on nongradedness, *The Improbable Form of Master Sturm.* Headmaster Johann Sturm established the first graded school in Strasbourg, Germany, in 1537. Students in Master Sturm's school spent a year in each class with a single teacher and completed a formal examination for promotion. Master Sturm's system seated pupils by age level on backless benches called *forms.* Six-year-olds were seated in the first form, 7-year-olds on the second form, and so on. This arrangement was carried to the United States in 1847 with the founding of the Quincy Grammar School in Boston. The vast majority of schools today still operate under these same conditions.

Why have these conditions prevailed? Surely interested persons both inside and outside education have done their best to make useful changes. Many recall the school improvement initiatives of the 1950s through 1980s, but it is not difficult to cite various reasons for the failure of these previous attempts at school restructuring. Schools and their clients have been remiss in vision, short on planning, lacking in certain resources, and careless in seeking broad support for their initiatives (Keefe, 1993). Dow (1973) suggested that the most fundamental cause of the failure is educators' lack of communication with the public, with other disciplines, with trends outside education. Educators are prone to work in isolation when most of the change needed in schooling requires outside help—from economists, political scientists, psychologists, sociologists, policymakers, and politicians.

Educators, and in particular school leaders, must begin to ask what kinds of schooling will effectively serve the society and the students of the 21st century. If we could imagine a *Time* magazine cover story on education in the year 2025, what kind of schooling would really merit that kind of attention? What approaches to organization, instruction, and learning would really move away from our medieval model of schooling?

In less than 50 years, our society has achieved an almost total shift from an industrial focus to an informational and service orientation. In 1950, more than 60% of the population earned a living by making something; less than 20% of the working force dealt with information or service. By 1980, manufacturing had dropped below 17% and information/service jobs passed the 65% mark. The shift continues to accelerate into the 1990s. This means that education and communication have assumed the central role in society that factories and banks held in the 1950s.

The purpose of education is to develop intelligence and skill in living. The schools that exist in much of the United States are rooted in the cultures and living skills of bygone societies. Our school schedules accommodate an agricultural society that we abandoned in the 1920s. Our school curricula and instruction reflect an industrial society of fixed periods of time, passive learning and lower order skills. The emerging information society requires flexible learners who are self-directed, capable of higher order thinking, and skilled in the technology of communication. These learners need schools that balance personal values with technological skills, that feature horizontal networks rather than vertical hierarchies, that provide wide variety in learning methodology yet ensure authentic instruction and learning. In a word, our emerging information society demands that schools move from collections of classrooms managed by teacher-presenters to flexible learning environments mentored by teacher-facilitators.

What can school leaders do about all of this? The sweeping nature of these needed changes calls for a comprehensive, indeed, a *systemic* approach to school leadership. Principals must begin to see their schools as complex systems dependent for success on many internal and external stakeholders. They must have real plans to guide school improvement—plans that are comprehensive, articulated, developed with the help of all stakeholders and pursued systematically. They must begin to view their schools as communities of learners, bound together by a common goal of student learning and growth, and committed to working collegially to achieve it.

Principals must begin to announce the "purpose story" of their schools. They must foster a visioning process, not just a vision document that can easily be laid aside, but the institutionalization of an ongoing process that involves all stakeholders in deciding what the school should be doing and in the resolve to carry it through.

Principals must again become instructional leaders—more than educational leaders, more than managers. They must become the mentors of their teaching staffs and the principal teachers of their schools.

This book explores the knowledge and skill base of Instruction and the Learning Environment (Domain 8) as proposed by the National Policy Board for Educational Administration (NPBEA) in *Principals for Our Changing Schools* (Thomson, 1993). Instruction and the Learning Environment is the first of the NPBEA's Programmatic Domains that focus on the scope and framework of the educational program. These domains "reflect the core technology of schools, instruction, and the related supporting services, developmental activities, and resource base"—the central processes of schooling. This book reviews current research and best practices in instruction and creating an effective learning environment. We focus on the elements of instructional leadership: creating a school culture for learning; envisioning and enabling with others appropriate initiatives for the improvement of teaching and learning; recognizing the developmental needs of students; ensuring appropriate instructional methods; helping to design positive learning experiences; accommodating student differences in cognition and achievement; and mobilizing all stakeholders to support these conditions for successful instruction and learning.

The most recent 10-year study of the high school principalship by the National Association of Secondary School Principals, *High School Leaders and Their Schools*, Volume II (Pellicer, et al., 1990) undertook a major investigation of instructional leadership. The study operationally defined instructional leadership as "the initiation and implementation of planned changes in a school's instructional program through the influence and direction of various constituencies in the school. Instructional leadership begins with an attitude, an expressed commitment to student productivity, from which emanates values, behaviors, and functions designed to foster student satisfaction and achievement." The study found that instructional leadership was a *shared responsibility*, not an administrative monopoly. Most commonly it was exercised by department chairpersons with the support of the school leadership team. It was *situational* and varied widely in style, vision and flexibility. It was a *planned experience*—in the absence of formal planning, nothing much happened. It was enhanced by a *common purpose* that was invariably student-centered and shared by all stakeholders. It was *risk-oriented*. The more persons engaged in risk-taking behavior, the more successful the outcomes. And it was characterized by *many informal behaviors*. It was strongly affective in intent and practice and clearly directed toward improving the instructional program.

The NASSP study points out the value of teamwork and collegiality in instructional leadership—the importance of planning, goal-direction, flexibility, and risk-orientation. The role of the principal and the school leadership team is central to this effort.

In the following chapters, we discuss the school learning organization, the meaning of learning, the elements of information processing theory, and the chief instructional models. We explore the elements of authentic pedagogy and cognitive-based learning environments in some depth. We summarize current thinking on subject matter instruction and assessment, instructional organization, and student motivation for learning. We conclude by reviewing contemporary approaches to action research.

1

THE SCHOOL AS A LEARNING ORGANIZATION

A national study of restructuring schools conducted by The Center on Organization and Restructuring of Schools (CORS) at the University of Wisconsin–Madison found that restructuring is most likely to succeed when changes in school organization are motivated by three principles: intellectual quality, community, and sustained effort (Newman, et al., 1995). Schools have tried various organizational reforms to improve student learning. Many have proved helpful—cooperative learning, detracking, higher academic standards, new forms of scheduling, personalization, performance-based assessment, school-site and shared decision-making, teaming—but the results ultimately have been disappointing because the primary effort has been directed to these technical aspects of schooling. The CORS study found that specific organizational reforms are more or less successful depending on the degree to which they reflect the three principles of intellectual quality, school community and sustained effort.

The first challenge in improving schools is to define high standards of intellectual quality for instruction and learning. Concern for the intellectual quality of student experiences involves developing curriculum with challenging content rather than just teaching to the text, and emphasizing cognitive processes that enable students to construct meaning and in-depth understanding from their learning experiences. Innovative teaching techniques can support intellectual quality, but only when linked to important intellectual goals and to standards for authentic teaching and learning. (We discuss authentic pedagogy, instruction, and assessment in greater detail in Chapter 4.)

The second challenge for school reform is building organizational capacity to achieve the defined standards of intellectual quality. The most basic purpose of school reform is not to create new structures or even to upgrade the competence of school personnel, but to improve the capacity of the entire school organization to support student intellectual outcomes. Schools improve their organizational capacity by becoming learning communities. They become learning *communities* when students and teachers see themselves clearly as learners, when they pursue shared intellectual goals, when they work collaboratively and take collective responsibility for learning, and when they have backing from all school stakeholders. (Newman, et al., 1995). School community, in turn, is strengthened when the school becomes a learning *organization*, continually expanding its capacity to create what its members mutually want to do. The foundation, as well as the mark of a functioning learning community and organization, is a unified school culture.

The third challenge of reform is to sustain the effort of school improvement. Schools jump from one educational fad to another with sparse provision for ongoing visioning, longitudinal analysis of results, or data-based planning. Schools are "programmed" to death, with little articulation among programs and no commitment to a sustained focus. Many schools implement improvements, but few institutionalize these reforms in the culture of the organization. Sustained effort requires continuity in district and school leadership and in teaching staff, a common vision and goals that are continually reviewed and updated, and support from all stakeholders—school community and parents, policy and political agencies, and independent reform organizations like the Accelerated Schools Project, the Coalition of Essential Schools, and the Learning Environments Consortium.

CREATING A LEARNING ORGANIZATION

Nevis, et al. (1995), describe organizational learning as "the capacity or process within an organization to maintain or improve performance based on experience." This capacity implies the existence of processes and structures for acquiring, sharing, and using knowledge and skills. Successful learning organizations typically share three characteristics that give them the organizational capacity for improvement:

♦ Well-developed *core competencies* that can lead to new products or services—In school organizations, core competencies include personnel policies and practices, staff development strategies, instructional delivery, and so on.

♦ *Attitudes* supportive of continuous improvement, the cultural norms and expectations that produce a positive school climate and a risk-free school environment—A successful school environment supports a challenging curriculum, authentic instruction and assessment, and good communication.

♦ The *capability to redesign and renew* the processes and structures of the organization—The successful instructional environment is flexible, personalized and committed to developing intellectual quality, school community and sustained effort.

In a recent interview (O'Neil, 1995), Peter Senge, the Director of the Center for Organizational Learning at the MIT Sloan School of Management, observed that most schools are not learning organizations because they are not places where people work together to create the things they want done. Schools are rule-based places in which teachers work alone and students are engaged primarily in memorizing things that are of little intellectual or practical use to them.

Senge goes on to say that it is difficult to support collective learning in schools. "The education enterprise is especially complicated because not only does the organization have different levels; it's very stratified. You've got teachers, principals, off-site administrators, school board members. I'm not convinced many of them see themselves as having a lot of power. . . . And so it really should come as very little surprise that it's almost incapable of innovation." Schools interested in creating learning organizations must concentrate on building environments where teachers can continuously learn. Senge suggests that principals start by bringing together those committed to a renewed school environment to talk to one another. Next, principals must create the most inclusive process possible under the circumstances to involve all interested parties in an ongoing "visioning" process—in deciding what they really want the school to become.

THE FIVE DISCIPLINES

Senge believes that a learning organization grows from a commitment to what he calls the five "learning disciplines" (Senge, 1990; Senge, et al., 1994). Each discipline is distinct, but together they build the learning organization.

BUILDING SHARED VISION

The first discipline is concerned with "visioning," with building shared images of the future of the school. Visioning is an ongoing process that brings all stakeholders together to construct what they want to do in the school. It is not just a "vision statement" that is framed and filed, but a conversation that empowers ongoing change in the school. It touches all aspects of school organization and instructional delivery.

PERSONAL MASTERY

The second discipline engages all members of the organization in developing and clarifying their personal visions and in helping to create an organization that supports each individual in mastering needed skills. Just as personal vision is the foundation of shared vision, so personal mastery is the basis for organizational development. Only when a school has a high percentage of administrators and teachers with broad mastery of educational skills can a truly successful learning organization be sustained. Shared vision and mastery begin to develop when individuals feel supported in their *personal* quests for mastery.

MENTAL MODELS

The third discipline involves confronting one's view of the world. We condition our judgments and actions by our mental models of reality; in this case, of the school and its learning environment. If we bring conventional views of schooling to the processes of visioning and personal mastery, if we believe that schooling should be as it was in the past, then we will try to recreate that reality. To achieve a functioning learning organization, a school must confront the differences in the mental models and personal visions of its members and then work to create a new consensus.

TEAM LEARNING

The fourth discipline postulates that teams, not individuals, are the fundamental units in modern organizations. Senge (1990) distinguishes between *discussion* and *dialogue* in developing team learning. Discussion is concerned with explaining a point of view in order to win an argument. Dialogue is a conversation that explores differences of opinion in order to resolve them. In most schools, discussion is the norm. Educators present and defend their views. Compromise, not consensus, is the goal. In a functioning learning organization, both discussion and dialogue are important. Discussion identifies differences and dialogue moves beyond them. As Senge (1990) puts it: "Individuals suspend their assumptions but they communicate their assumptions freely. . . . In dialogue, people become observers of their own thinking."

SYSTEMS THINKING

The fifth discipline is a conceptual framework that integrates team learning, mental models, personal mastery and shared vision. It is a body of knowledge and tools that help a learning organization understand its patterns of operation and how they can be changed. A system is a group of components that operate together and influence the operation of the whole. Human bodies are systems. A modern building is a system. Automobiles are systems. The first principle of systems thinking is that "structure influences behavior." A system functions in a certain way because of its structures. In a very real way, a system causes its own behavior. Conventional schools, for example, function in traditional ways because their system components make it hard to do otherwise. The systemic structure of a school is the pattern of relationships, not among the people, but among the key components of the school organization. (See Keefe and Howard, in press.)

Peter Senge (1990) discusses eleven laws of systems thinking in *The Fifth Discipline: The Art and Practice of the Learning Organization*. The following examples suggest some of the implications of these laws:

♦ *The harder you push, the harder the system pushes back*. This is *compensating feedback* in systems thinking. The harder you try, the harder success seems to be. Schools that attempt to personalize the instructional environment discover all the student needs that have been ignored in the past.

♦ *The easy way out usually leads back in*. Familiar or time-honored solutions to issues or problems may actually make them worse. Problem learners are given bigger doses of what they do poorly in the first place (more lectures, more seatwork, more tests).

♦ *Cause and effect are not closely related in time and space*. Complicated problems have complex explanations; the prime causes often are quite remote from the effects. Poor student achievement may reflect poor motivation or study habits, but the ultimate explanation may be an unresponsive curriculum or boring instruction.

♦   *Small changes can produce big results—but the areas of highest leverage are often the least obvious.* Solving a complicated problem requires finding the point of greatest leverage, where the least effort can make the biggest difference. The points of highest leverage are usually not obvious. Most schools fail to help problem learners because they neither diagnose their cognitive/learning styles nor remediate their poor learning skills. Instead they often place them in a repeated cycle of failure.

♦   *There is no blame.* In systems thinking, the system itself is the problem, not the people. If the components of the systems are dysfunctional, problems will arise. No one in or outside the system is to blame. The *system* itself must be changed to effect a solution. Urban schools, for example, are thought to be the victims of poor teachers and unruly students when the reality is that the structures and/or processes of these schools cannot support student learning. To sustain real improvement, the system must be modified and all system components brought into synchronization.

School as Community

The school cannot become a total learning organization until it becomes a "community of learners." Community is necessary because students need a supportive learning environment, one that is virtually risk-free, to pursue standards of high intellectual quality. Community makes it more likely that students will work with adults, do the hard work necessary for intellectual growth, and take the risks needed for real reflection, sustained conversation, and higher order thinking. Community also provides the social and technical support that teachers need to renew the learning environment.

Lee, Croninger, and Smith (1995) have studied three organizational characteristics of high schools as learning communities. Two of these characteristics, staff cooperation and teacher empowerment, showed no *direct* effect on student achievement and engagement over the first 2 years of high school. These variables, however, were highly correlated with a third—collective responsibility for learning. The Lee, et al., studies showed that collective responsibility for student learning is positively related to gains in student achievement, both early and late in high school. It is also related to a more equitable distribution of achievement.

In addition, the researchers found that students learn more, and learning is more equitably distributed in schools, where students take more academic courses, where they take much the same courses, where student and teacher morale is high, and where teachers and students place high priority on learning and achievement (academic press).

Collective responsibility for student learning, an academic emphasis and high morale, then, are important features of a successful school learning community. In a similar vein, a school-based professional community (Kruse & Seashore Louis, 1995) works to integrate teacher professionalism and organizational community. Teachers strive to increase collective responsibility for student performance. This kind of school-based professional community is characterized by:

- *Reflective dialogue*—teachers engage in serious conversations about educational issues and student learning problems;
- *Deprivatization of practice*—teachers frequently examine their teaching behaviors, observe other teachers, and share strategies for improvement;
- *Collective focus on student learning*—teachers are more concerned about outcomes than strategies, with student performance than teaching techniques;

♦ *Collaboration in professional development*—teachers work together regularly to improve professional skills and the organization of the learning environment;

♦ *Shared norms and values*—teachers are committed to developing a school-based professional community and to the disciplines of a learning organization.

Kruse and Seashore Louis (1995) argue that various conditions and resources support the development of this community. Important *structural conditions* include time to meet and talk, small size, physical proximity, team teaching, regular meetings and convenient communication structures (e-mail), school autonomy and school-based management, and building-level selection and control of personnel. Critical *social and human conditions* include staff openness to improvement and willingness to accept feedback, an atmosphere of trust and respect, an adequate knowledge and skill base for effective teaching and learning, supportive leadership, and an intensive socialization process. In short, the school culture must be collaborative, risk-free, focused on student learning, and committed to a systems approach to personal and organizational improvement.

SCHOOL CULTURE AND CLIMATE

A prerequisite to school-based professional community and organizational learning is a responsive school culture. Stolp and Smith (1995, p. 11) define culture as "historically transmitted patterns of meaning that include the norms, beliefs, traditions, and myths understood, maybe in varying degrees, by members of the school community." Culture encompasses the daily rituals and important ceremonies of a school: its subcultures, and its underlying values, beliefs, and assumptions. The least tangible level of a school culture involves beliefs about the nature of learners and learning, the purposes of schooling, and the basic organizational design. Schools that aspire to become learning organizations and school-based professional communities must reflect values like "all students can successfully learn," "teachers accept collective responsibility for student learning," and "learners are all different and have a right to respect, fairness and caring in the school."

A supportive school culture is distinguished by subcultures and common practices that support a learning community. Subcultural norms such as academic orientation and dress and grooming must function in a true learning organization in harmony with the mission and goals of the school. Common practices must support academic excellence, mutual respect, and caring, honesty, and integrity, fairness and equity, etc. All ceremonies and rituals of the school must reinforce the value of learning as a means towards a satisfying and successful life. Rewards and recognition ceremonies such as honor rolls, trophies and athletic awards must emphasize the major values to which the school is committed.

Climate is one of the major descriptors of school culture. The NASSP Task Force on School Environments (Keefe, Kelley, & Miller, 1985) defines school climate as "the relatively enduring pattern of shared perceptions of the characteristics of a school and of its members." A school culture that supports a school learning organization will reflect a positive school climate. All major stakeholders—students, teachers, parents and community—will view the school environment in a positive fashion. The shared perceptions of all these stakeholders will validate the academic orientation of the school, its sense of collective responsibility and the sustained commitment to students and their learning. Measures of the school climate will show that teachers are fair to students, that students know why they are in school, and that the community backs the school in its mission and vision. Teachers will report support of their attempts to improve the learning environment. Students will feel that they are making sense of what they are learning.

CONSTRUCTIVISM AND CRITICAL PEDAGOGY

Constructivism is a contemporary epistemology that holds that human beings construct knowledge by giving meaning to current experiences in the light of prior knowledge. "Knowledge construction occurs within individuals who themselves are a part of a community that shares knowledge via verbal and nonverbal means. The social construction of knowledge in a culture involves negotiation and consensus building among the members of the culture" (Tobin & Fraser, 1991). A school structured on a constructivist epistemology stresses that students should make meaning of what they are learning. Students construct their own meaning quite naturally. The learning environment, appropriately organized, expands the process and deepens understanding.

A key to this kind of meaning-making is time and opportunity for reflective discussion and dialogue. Students need time to interact with teachers and their peers. Instruction builds on students' information processing skills and learning styles. Teachers attempt to personalize instruction as much as possible, de-emphasizing traditional strategies such as lecture-discussion, seatwork, and utilizing self-directed approaches like computer assisted instruction, reciprocal teaching, cooperative learning, long-term projects, and seminars. Students are encouraged to seek out knowledge wherever it can best be found (library, museum, database, expert). These resources are used by students to *construct knowledge*, with the help of their teachers and other mentors. They work with teachers to improve their information processing (thinking) skills and use these cognitive strategies to clarify, analyze, extrapolate, and form consensus about important knowledge.

D.C. Phillips (1995) suggests that "there is a broad and loose sense in which all of us these days are constructivists. . . ." Most of us do not believe that knowledge is acquired ready-made, nor that everyone possesses the cognitive skill to construct all the knowledge needed for a productive life. John Dewey (1988/1929) said it well: "Ideas are worthless except as they pass into actions which rearrange and reconstruct in some way, be it little or large, the world in which we live." Meaning is made as prior knowledge is connected with current experience through reflection. This connection broadens and expands the experience of the learner. Teaching involves connecting a given group of learners with important experiences and with powerful ideas that can expand the experiences, and helping link these processes to the prior experiences of the learners. Prawat (1995) reminds us that Dewey's approach represents "idea-based social constructivism" which "assigns highest priority to ideas developed within the academic disciplines."

The task of instruction within idea-based social constructivism is to create learning communities that allow students to confront big ideas, such as an author's view in a significant work, and to apply these views to real-world experiences that the learner can understand and use. Prawat (1995) sees the classroom, or more precisely, the learning environment, as the center of discourse "where people engage in animated conversations about important intellectual matters." Teachers work with students to generate ideas and students work to validate the ideas for themselves, using them to explain aspects of the real world that otherwise they would not perceive or understand. This process is the substance of a professional learning community and its school learning organization. A constructivist epistemology, in turn, is an ideal foundation on which to build a school learning organization.

A commitment to "critical pedagogy" is a good place to begin this quest. Critical pedagogy is a process that examines and evaluates the dominant values underlying a school's instructional system to ensure that all students benefit. It asks whose norms are being taught and whose culture is being promoted.

All instructional programs and related strategies assume certain values and cultural norms. "Critical pedagogy seeks to create a 'level playing field' for all students. It recognizes the diversity that children bring to the school and respects the many cultures and perspectives that exist in an increasingly multicultural society" (English, Keefe, et al., 1993). Schools mirror larger social relationships and reflect them in their daily practices and common rituals. Schooling is value laden and can easily perpetuate existing inequities based on socioeconomic differences or student skill deficiencies. A school learning organization must strive to broaden its cultural focus and to enable all students to grow.

TOWARD A LEARNING ORGANIZATION

The path to a school learning organization is illustrated in Figure 1.1. An inclusive school culture and a constructivist epistemology engender a school-based professional community that makes possible the growth of the five learning disciplines and the competencies, attitudes, and sustained commitment of a school learning organization.

FIGURE 1.1. PATHWAY TO A SCHOOL LEARNING ORGANIZATION

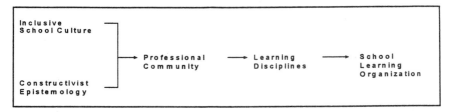

Learning organizations obviously take time to build, but the first steps can be taken immediately. The most basic step is to support an inclusive school culture encompassing a personalized approach to teaching and learning and a learning environment that promotes the making of meaning. This teaching-learning environment must be relatively risk-free and conducive to self-directed learning. School leaders, in particular, must make personal time to think and reflect, to assess the cogency of current school programs, and to involve all school stakeholders in reflective dialogue. Systemic change demands attention to all the components of the organization at the same time. It is the responsibility of the school leadership team to initiate and sustain this process and commitment.

ACTION STEPS

- ♦ Read Peter Senge's book, *The Fifth Discipline: The Art and Practice of the Learning Organization* (Doubleday/Currency, New York, 1990). Assess the degree to which your school is committed to the five disciplines of the learning organization.

♦ Convene a group of representative stakeholders from your school (administrators, teachers, students, parents, community leaders) to initiate a "visioning process." If this is not feasible, meet with an interested group of colleagues. Through discussion and dialogue, determine what you want your school to be and do for its students in the next decade. Frame an initial (working) vision statement.

♦ Consider your school and decide what areas in your structure, organization and program constitute the highest points of leverage for school improvement—where the least effort can make the biggest difference. Form a school task force to pursue the agreed upon strategies for improvement.

♦ Analyze the dominant values underlying your school's instructional system. Does your school operate as a learning community where teachers engage frequently in reflective dialogue and share a *collective* focus on student learning and performance? Does your school have a supportive culture that rewards learning and academic excellence? Do school stakeholders perceive the school climate to be positive and committed to students and their learning? Assess your school climate using NASSP's School Climate Survey (1904 Association Drive, Reston, VA 22091, 703-860-0200).

♦ Make time in your schedule to think and reflect about the cogency of your current school programs. Involve school stakeholders in reflective dialogue about the most effective *design* for your school of the future.

2

LEARNING AND INFORMATION PROCESSING

Students go to school to learn. The question is what and how they learn. Perhaps that is not really the first question. Rather, we should ask what is meant by "learning." A misunderstanding and limited meaning of the word have bedeviled practitioners for decades. For many, learning means memorizing, and teaching, accordingly, means expounding in such a way that memorization is facilitated.

But learning is not simply memorizing. In education, we know that learning has taken place when a learner evidences a change of behavior of a more or less permanent nature resulting from what has been experienced. The learner behaves differently from the way he or she did previously. But not all learning is evident. We must often infer higher conceptual or affective learning from secondary behaviors; for example, music appreciation from concert attendance. In any case, what has been learned has not just been memorized; it has been assimilated so that future acts may change as a result. To learn, then, is to adopt a new and enhanced response to a situation.

Learning is an active process involving the many powers of the learner. The emphasis upon different powers varies according to the matter to be learned, and the maturity of the learner. Thus a young child's thinking toward a solution will be based on the results of physical action, whereas older adolescents and adults tend to respond more verbally and mentally.

Learning is essentially an individual affair, affected by the learner's personality characteristics, stage of mental development, the needs and drives which motivate him, the influence of her personal environment, and so on. Teaching, today, recognizing this deeper aspect of learning, does not expect all children to learn in the same way. This realization of differential response is a prime factor in the transformation of a classroom from a *teaching* environment to a *learning* one.

A further problem exists with a too close association of learning with memorization. We can only memorize things that are or have been. Yet one of the most important purposes of education is to equip students of all ages with the tools necessary to face their own individual futures confidently. This confrontation involves solving problems; and so problem solving in the school is essential if it is to be a preparation for life. Indeed, what has been personally solved or discovered is much more likely to be retained than something simply accepted by rote or reading.

This is not to suggest that memorization is useless; it can save time and effort. In its rote-learning sense, however, it is much less important than it was. We must not expect too much of it. One of the major criticisms of traditional school testing is that it overemphasizes memory and leaves too many other qualities untested. Much of what is learned is highly personal and difficult to examine. Learning is special to each student and is affected by the qualities that the individual brings to the learning situation.

BACKGROUND HISTORY

The modern study of learning began in the final decades of the 19th century with the work of Wilhelm Wundt (Germany) and William James (Harvard). Wundt emphasized experimental psychology, measuring the amount of time required to perform various mental operations and translating everyday experiences into measurable units. James was at heart a philosopher and writer. He described and interpreted the new science of learning and spelled out its implications for educators. James' theory of learning included the following principles (Farnham-Diggory, 1992):

♦ Learning should begin with a central theme, "some deep aspect" around which ideas can collect.

♦ Learning must produce behavior; it must be active and put to immediate use.

♦ Learning is the process of substituting one response for another; e.g., a polite or sophisticated response for an impulsive one.

♦ Learning is the formation of associations; teaching is the building up of associations in the learner.

Many of William James' principles of learning are quite contemporary and still influence scholars of learning. Attempts to build a modern science of school learning would surely have developed more quickly had these principles continued to inform the ongoing discussion at the beginning of this century. Yet, from World War I to about 1950, behaviorism, not William James, prevailed.

Behaviorism is about measurement. Wilhelm Wundt had emphasized that for psychology to be a science, things had to be measured. What to measure was the challenge. Much of what people learn is not visible except in its manifestations. Wundt could measure the speed of a subject's reaction time to some stimulus, but other, more subtle learning could be inferred only from external behavior. Psychologists turned to the study of animal behavior. A succession of behaviorists from Thorndike to Pavlov to Watson studied "stimulus" and "response" (S-R). But these early behaviorists were unwilling to move from identifying responses to inferring the mental actions that linked stimulus with response. Some 50 years passed before important cognitive aspects were again admitted to the serious study of psychology and learning.

The cognitive movement in psychology began with the *Gestalt* school of thought in Germany before World War II. In 1923, Max Wertheimer proposed six *Gestalt* laws of perceptual organization which stressed that the *relationships* among parts established the whole. A tune, for example, can be identified in any key because the relationships among the notes remain constant. In problem solving and learning, the internal relationships or patterns are the key to understanding.

Cognitive science was successively enriched by the works of such psychologists as Kurt Lewin (Field Theory), Edward Tolman (Purposive Behaviorism), James Gibson (Unified Sensation and Perception), Noam Chomsky (Transformational Grammar), Jerome Bruner (Study of Thinking), and George Miller, Eugene Galanter, and Karl Pribram (Plans and the Structure of Behavior). By the late 1950s, psychologists were thinking and speaking less of stimulus-response and more of information processing to describe the complicated ways that human beings think, learn and solve problems.

Computer technology also opened new theoretical doors. "The new technology made new psychological theories possible—theories that are much more complex and interesting than S-R theories. Because of the computer, we can finally unpack the hyphen. We can spread on the table all sorts of marvelous ideas about the stream of mental processes that are activated by a stimulus and that generate the response. And we can at last get on with the important business of investigating the conditions that expedite cognition—the conditions of good instruction." (Farnham-Diggory, 1992, p. 46). Computer paradigms enabled psychologists to construct new simulations of mental processes and to overturn the crudest forms of behaviorism. Howard Gardner (1985) aptly summarizes the work of the cognitivists in *The Mind's New Science*. Cognitive science is based on the belief that information can be mentally represented, manipulated, and studied. (Behaviorism alleged exactly the opposite.) This new science is interdisciplinary, rooted in philosophy, and uses the computer as its basic tool. It proposes a new structure or architecture of thinking and learning.

INFORMATION PROCESSING THEORY

Cognitive psychology is concerned with information processing—what human beings do when they think and learn. Differences of opinion do exist about the exact structures of the mind, what computer scientists call its "system architecture," but general agreement exists on three basic structures: (a) Perceptual Systems (also called Information or Start-Up Systems), (b) Short-Term or Working Memory, and (c) Long-Term Memory (see Fig. 2.1).

FIGURE 2.1. THE HUMAN INFORMATION PROCESSING SYSTEM

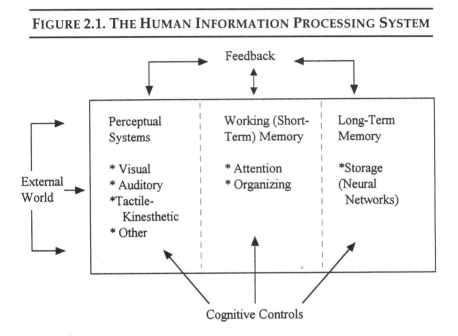

PERCEPTUAL SYSTEMS

Information coming from the actual world is held briefly in perceptual or trace memories (sometimes called buffers). During the ¼ to 4 or 5 seconds of trace memory, the working memory decides whether the information is important and whether to reject, memorize, transform, or learn it. For example, a person sees a picture or hears a sound. The information is held in *iconic* (visual) or *echoic* (auditory) memory briefly while working (short-term) memory attends to it. This is the startup phase.

In fact, there are five human perceptual systems for collection of information from external reality. These systems are the visual, the auditory, the tactual-kinesthetic or haptic, the taste-smell, and the basic orienting system (balance). It is no longer very meaningful to talk about the five (or more) senses because the current scientific discussion admits to many kinds of sensitive cells or receptors in all these perceptual systems. Each system is active in gathering information. The visual system, for example, includes light-sensitive cells in the retina, the structure of the eye, and a complex set of muscles. It is basically a scanning system that searches for information. The auditory system, by contrast, has much less capacity to scan the environment. Humans seem to have a primary visual orientation toward the environment (along with other primates).

The haptic system includes tactual receptors in the skin and receptors in the muscles and joints. Examining an object is much more than just touching it. Handling involves movement and information about shape which is picked up by the receptors in the muscles and joints (Travers, 1982).

The taste-smell and basic orienting (balance) systems have only small relevance to school-related learning.

WORKING MEMORY

Working or short-term memory is the least understood of the memory systems although much experimental work has been devoted to it (in studying verbal learning). All information must enter the short-term system before it can become a part of the learner's cognitive structure (long-term memory). Typically, working memory is conceptualized as the location where information is stored before long-term storage. Various conceptualizations see it as a store from which information is selected for transfer to long-term memory, or as that aspect of memory of which we are conscious, or as the perceptual process that includes all sensory inputs and the interpretation of these inputs through information stored in long-term memory (Watkins, 1974).

Attention is the link between perception and working memory. Attention involves focusing and taking information from some particular aspect of the environment. Beyond general scanning, attention concentrates on detail. When a teacher supervises students engaged in seatwork, or independent projects, she merely scans the group. But when she sees a student having difficulty (or misbehaving), she focuses on (attends to) that student. The act of attending is always complex. The working memory can contend with only a few items of information at any given instant. To provide continuity, it compiles and implements *mental programs* that link one act of attending to another. Working memory ties the past to the present, enabling the learner to integrate new information into the existing cognitive structure.

Information is *organized* in memory by means of working programs that persist over time. When a student wants to learn something, he or she at least implicitly establishes a goal. This goal triggers a mental plan with subgoals, associated knowledge, skills, images, etc., and activates that knowledge in long-term memory. Working memory reminds the learner of relevant sensory cues (location of resources, study areas, environment) and directs and monitors behavior towards the goal. It also monitors its own operations, keeping track of progress and terminating the mental program when the goal is no longer active. "As you go through the day, one goal after another assembles one program after another in your working memory. All the programs are composed of *symbols* for (a) goals; (b) knowledge; (c) sensory cues; (d) behavior; and (e) progress checks. These are the *basic components* of working memory programs" (Farnham-Diggory, 1992, p. 67).

Many working memory programs run automatically—you do not have to think about them. And many programs run at the same time; they are embedded within larger programs. Computer science refers to this sharing capability as *timesharing*. Working memory distributes its information processing capability by placing some programs on hold while it runs others or by running some programs automatically while it monitors others.

Some learners are better at this than others. Those with poor organizational skills have trouble keeping track. Skilled learners construct higher-order working memory programs to manage and monitor other mental programs. They also perfect their cognitive control skills. (More about this later.)

Maintenance time and storage in working memory is limited. It can be increased by extended practice ("overlearning") and through such mnemonic devices as "chunking" and grouping.

Chunking reduces the number of pieces of information that must be maintained and adds organization to the process. It is as easy to retain and recall three-word expressions as single words. The material is learned in chunks. This added level of meaning makes the information easier to organize and provides cues for recall. Traditional chunking strategies include the infamous "Roy G. Biv" to organize and recall the primary colors of red (R), Orange (O), yellow (Y), green (G), blue (B), indigo (I), and violet (V). Music education uses the phrase "Every Good Boy Does Fine" for the lines of the staff (EGBDF) and the word "FACE" for the spaces. Working memory's most important function is to maintain and organize information in such a way that real learning (not just memorization) can occur in long-term memory.

LONG-TERM MEMORY

Long-term memory is the repository of previously learned information, propositions, and hierarchical networks of reconstructed knowledge. Learners must move information from the working memory to the long-term memory in order to incorporate it in their cognitive structures for later recall and/or modification. Information in long-term memory must be adequately organized if it is to be recalled. Imagine the difficulty of finding something in an encyclopedia if it were not alphabetically arranged. But the human mind is much more complex than an encyclopedia or even a computer. The ability to store and rapidly recall important information has contributed to man's historical survival. It is a key characteristic of the human brain.

Many theories have been developed to explain how long-term memory is organized. Travers (1982) mentions six theories going back to the time of Aristotle:

- ◆ *Classical theory* proposes that long-term memory (LTM) is a system of ideas linked by associations into a complex network. Modern studies of word association carry on this tradition.

- ◆ The *hierarchical model* suggests that LTM is composed of specific ideas categorized under more general ideas. Men and apes can be categorized under primates, and primates under animals.

- The *propositional model* (Kintsch & Keenan, 1973) postulates that long-term *semantic* memory is structured as essential ideas and representations of meaning. Propositions are not stored literally but in a kind of short hand that holds the essential meaning. This theory best suits adult verbal memory; children's memory does not seem to be propositional.

- *Schema or schemes* were formulated by the neurologist Henry Head and elaborated by Jean Piaget. Piaget said that infant behavior was organized around innate reflexes that included both perceptual and response components. Later behavior is organized around ideas.

- *Episodic and semantic* memory systems were suggested by Tulving (1972). Long-term episodic memory stores the events and happenings of a person's life. Long-term semantic memory stores general knowledge—pieces of information such as words, meanings, relationships, rules, formulas, etc. (None of this information is situation specific.)

- *Attribute theory* proposes that long-term memory is the storage of attributes (the characteristics of experiences) and information about how they are combined. Considerable evidence supports the nature of memory as a series of attributes but how the attributes are related is still highly speculative.

Long-term memory contains virtually everything we have ever learned (semantic information) or experienced (episodic information) in a more or less accessible and organized fashion. For information to be organized in long-term memory in a way that it can be easily retrieved, three conditions must be met. Information must be (a) actually learned, (b) organized while being learned, and (c) integrated into existing cognitive structures (Letteri, 1988). The working memory exercises various executive functions together with long-term memory to control the final disposition of information. Four decisions can be made at any stage from perceptual memory to long-term storage: to reject, to transform, to memorize, to learn.

TO REJECT

Information may be rejected either in an automatic or controlled fashion. Information may be received but not attended to because the learner is thinking about something else. Driving a car, for example, depends on many automatic actions. We drive safely without attending to many of the steps. We can also reject at will. Students do this all the time in classrooms when they tune out the teacher for their own thoughts. Rejected information is lost.

TO TRANSFORM

Transformation occurs when information is incorrectly identified and processed as if it were something else. The original information is erroneously changed into something else. This may consist in selecting only a part of the information or only familiar information, and rejecting the rest. It may also involve assuming that *new* information is already known. In either event, transformation results in a compromised cognitive structure and makes retrieval of information difficult or impossible.

TO MEMORIZE

Memorization is the most common information processing decision and is generally confused with real *learning*. Memorization is *not* real learning. The latter demands that new information add to or modify existing information in long-term memory. Memorizing involves two strategies: maintenance rehearsal and elaborative rehearsal. Maintenance rehearsal is useful when information is needed only for a very short time (remembering a telephone number to dial it). This level of rehearsal retains only a small amount of information (3–5 pieces) for a brief interval (several minutes). Drill and practice sessions exemplify this process in schools. Elaborative rehearsal involves the application of specific organizational structures to information so that it can be sorted and retrieved from long-term memory. Mnemonics and chunking are the most common elaborative strategies. Memorized information does not add to or modify existing categories in a learner's long-term memory.

TO LEARN

Learning is a decision to enhance or modify the existing cognitive structure. Learning requires the learner to control the processing of information. When presented with new information, the learner must analyze its features, scan existing information in long-term memory for a category with the same features and, if found, add the data to the existing category. If no category exists, a new one must be created. Learning is a conscious, controlled and directed activity (Letteri, 1988).

COGNITIVE CONTROLS

Various cognitive skills facilitate information processing. The early work on cognitive controls proceeded from research in personality theory. In particular, the work of Gordon Allport and L.L. Thurstone supported the concepts of cognitive controls and cognitive styles. Allport and Vernon's *Studies in Expressive Movement* (1933) were an attempt to define personality constraints in cognitive processing. Thurstone's (1944) factorial study of perceptual behavior assumed that perception is dependent in part on information processing controls that influence the operation of the system. Cognitive controls are processing skills that affect and place limitations on cognitive processing. These controls influence both motivation to learn and response to environmental stimuli. Individual differences in cognitive behavior may reflect different ways of coping with reality. Gardner, et al. (1959, p. 5) put it this way:

> Cognitive controls are conceived of as slow-changing, developmentally stabilized structures: (a) they are relatively invariant over a given class of situations and intentions; (b) they are operative despite the shifts in situational and behavioral contexts typical of cognitive

activity from moment to moment. Cognitive controls refer to a level of organization that is more general than the specific structural components underlying perception, recall and judgment.

Each learner employs a number of cognitive controls at varying levels of skill. The composite of controls in any individual influences cognitive behavior in a way that could not be predicted from the characteristics of any one control. This composite of controls is a learner's cognitive style.

Samuel Messick and his associates (1976) discuss some 20 cognitive controls dealing with perception and concept attainment. Letteri (1976) and others have concentrated on 7 to 10 controls that seem to have the most significant relationship to students' academic achievement. Letteri found that successful students are more analytic, focused, reflective, accurate, complex, tolerant of ambiguity, and capable of discrete memorization. Letteri (1985) offers these definitions of the seven controls in his Cognitive Profile:

- ◆ *Analytic* (field dependence-independence)—the skill required to segment complex information into component parts for the purposes of identification and categorization.

- ◆ *Focusing* (scanning)—the skill required to selectively attend to one relevant component without being distracted by other relevant components.

- ◆ *Comparative analysis* (reflectiveness-impulsiveness)—the skill required to select a correct response from among several highly similar, but nonidentical alternatives, and to perform a highly accurate and properly ordered comparison between two or more pieces of information.

- ◆ *Narrow* (breadth of categorization)—the accuracy and consistency of category placement of new information in long-term memory. Category placement refers to the network of categories that exist in an individual's long-term memory.

- *Complex* (complexity-simplicity)—the arrangement and integration of information into cognitive structures. Complexity governs the form and the structure of all categories of information in long-term memory.

- *Sharpening* (sharpening-leveling)—the skill required to maintain distinctions between different data and ideas in processing information and to avoid confusing or overlapping them. Sharpening is essential in identifying and categorizing new information as well as in its retrieval from long-term memory.

- *Tolerance* (tolerant - intolerant)—the skill required to engage in and monitor the modification of cognitive structures, and to examine apparently ambiguous information. Tolerance of ambiguity is necessary for any modification to occur in cognitive structures.

The National Task Force on Learning Style supported by the National Association of Secondary School Principals also identified sequential and simultaneous processing as important cognitive controls (See Keefe & Monk, 1988).

- *Sequential processing*—a learner's capability or bias for processing information in a step-by-step, linear fashion. Verbal processing is sequential, but any step-by-step process, like mathematical computation, qualifies.

- *Simultaneous processing*—a learner's capability or bias for integrating the separate elements of experience into a whole or gestalt. Simultaneous processing often has a strong visual or spatial component, as well as a relational thinking component; i.e., perceiving an overall pattern from the relationships among the parts.

Research supports the operation of various cognitive controls in information processing. Cognitive controls operate together and at every stage of the information processing system. They influence the flow of new information through the system, feedback within the system, the accuracy of information retrieval, and ultimately, the accuracy of learner performance based on that information.

THE LEARNING PROCESS

What then is learning from the perspective of information processing theory? Phye and Andre propose four important features of the process (reprinted with the permission of Academic Press, Inc., from *Cognitive Classroom Learning—Understanding, Thinking and Problem Solving*, by Gary D. Phye and Thomas Andre, 1986, pp. 11–12).

1. Information to be learned must be attended to.
2. Information to be learned is processed through a series of stages into more complex forms.
3. The representation formed of the information is determined both by the information itself (bottom-up processing) and by the previous general schemata of the student (top-down processing). This means that what a student acquires from instruction is determined as much by what the student already knows as by the nature of the instruction.
4. Using previous knowledge to elaborate upon the presented information facilitates its transfer into long-term memory. . . When the student relates new information to old information already in long-term memory, the student is more likely to learn and remember the new information. In addition, the way in which the student processes the new information determines the nature of the representation formed in memory and the way in which the new information can be used.

The learning process begins with selective attention to relevant information and a selective ignoring of other information. The skills that the student then brings to the process of encoding, elaborating on and categorizing the information influence the degree to which the information will be remembered and later retrieved in relevant situations. The degree to which the student processes information for meaning, relates it to information previously stored in long-term memory, and engages in elaborative strategies (incorporating it in a story or using mnemonics) enhances the student's learning and retention.

In the past, cognitive science was concerned primarily with describing cognitive processes, but the focus today is more on how cognitive skills are acquired, on knowledge acquisition, conceptual development, and skills in problem-solving. Sternberg (1985) reminds us that an information-processing approach to human abilities arose during the past 20 years as an attempt to better understand individual differences. Psychometricians have tended to stress the *structure* of the intellect. Information-processing psychologists are more interested in the *processes* that underlie intelligence. Psychometricians start with individual differences in order to study intellectual functioning; information-processing psychologists start with how learners perform on tasks and then look for individual differences. Many in the latter group now agree that intelligence is a set of information-processing skills that can be diagnosed and taught.

Sternberg (1982) suggests that such skills include problem identification, the selection of relevant information sources and ways to organize and represent information, the choice of sequencing strategies, allocation of time, monitoring of progress, receiving of feedback, and translating feedback into an action plan and implementing it. These skills imply that diagnosis is a key element of successful learning (together with organization and planning). Diagnosis of student cognitive control skills is fundamental to this kind of assessment, followed by the careful retraining of student skill deficiencies and systematic instruction.

STYLE-BASED LEARNING AND INSTRUCTION

The central issue facing practitioners is how to improve the learning and achievement of students. To do this, school leaders and teachers must understand the principles of information processing, the influence of cognitive control skills on successful processing, and the importance of giving training and practice to students in controlling, directing and monitoring their information processing systems. Wittrock's (1985) model of generative learning supports the concept that individuals construct their own meaning based on "what the learner knows and what learning strategies the learner possesses." Learning style-related instruction fits well with information processing theory and what we know from neurophysiology about how the human brain responds to the learning environment.

Learning style is a construct that links perceptual response tendencies, cognitive control skills and study and instructional preferences. The NASSP Learning Styles Task Force defined learning style as "the composite of characteristic cognitive, affective and physiological factors that serve as relatively stable indicators of how a learner perceives, interacts with, and responds to the learning environment. It is demonstrated in that pattern of behavior and performance by which an individual approaches educational experiences. Its basis lies in the structure of neural organization and personality which both molds and is molded by human development and the learning experiences of home, school and society (Keefe & Languis, 1983). Task Force factor analytic research identified 24 significant perceptual responses, cognitive control skills, and study or instructional preferences that form the construct of learning style. Existing research suggests that students with particularly strong or particularly weak perceptual response patterns, cognitive control skills, and study/instructional preferences benefit from learning arrangements that support these tendencies. Students with strong analytic skills, for example, are ready for challenging instruction and can work at or beyond grade level in most subject areas. Students with weak analytic skills need skill enhancement before they can learn with confidence and useful retention of content.

Keefe (1991) outlines eight steps for planning style-based learning and instruction:

1. Diagnosing student learning styles with a generic instrument (like the NASSP Learning Style Profile) that

assesses perceptual, cognitive and study/instructional styles.

2. Profiling class or group tendencies and preferences to assist in planning instruction.

3. Determining significant group strengths and weaknesses to identify areas that may need skill enhancement or to develop projects for enrichment and special interest.

4. Examining subject content in the curriculum for areas that may create problems for learners with cognitive skill deficiencies.

5. Analyzing prior student achievement and performance for patterns of weakness that may reflect cognitive skill deficiencies.

6. Enhancing (Letteri calls it "augmenting") weak student cognitive skills using strategies like those suggested in the *Learning Style Profile Handbook,* Volume I (Jenkins, Letteri, & Rosenlund, 1990).

7. Reviewing current instructional methods and the organization of the school learning environment to determine whether these elements are adequate or demand more flexibility.

8. Modifying the learning environment and developing personalized student learning experiences like those suggested in the *Learning Style Profile Handbook,* Volume II (Keefe, 1989).

The first five steps are diagnostic and provide the basis for a carefully designed instructional plan. Step six requires that student cognitive deficiencies be remediated ("augmented"), either by setting up a clinical center in the school staffed by a trained cognitive specialist, or by training individual classroom teachers to assist students who have weak cognitive skills. Steps 7 and 8 involve a careful review of the existing learning environment and teaching methodologies in order to determine their suitability for the current student body. If needed, these processes may be systematically modified to adapt instruction to the way learners perform on learning tasks.

Style-based assessment is a starting point for successful instruction because it allows the teacher to base instructional practice on sound diagnostic information about the skills and needs of individual students. Knowing the strengths and weaknesses of students complements an information processing approach. If differential needs exist, then the tasks and processes of instruction can be appropriately fine-tuned.

ACTION STEPS

- Behaviorism is concerned primarily with measurement. Consider several traditional schools that you know well. Determine what influence this behaviorist emphasis on measurement has had on the organization and delivery of instruction in these schools.

- Reflect on the difference between memorization and real learning. Investigate approaches to higher order thinking skills such as *Tactics for Thinking* (McREL) that emphasize information processing and critical thinking rather than memorization. (*Cf. Tactics for Thinking* by Robert J. Marzano and Daisy E. Arredondo published by the Association for Supervision and Curriculum Development, Alexandria, VA, 1986.)

- Obtain a Sampler Kit of the NASSP *Learning Style Profile*. Administer the Profile to a small group of students and analyze their cognitive strengths and weaknesses. Develop a plan to help students improve their cognitive controls.

- Read Robert Sternberg's book, *Human Abilities: An Information Processing Approach* (W.H. Freeman, 1985). Determine whether your school's instructional approach incorporates training of students in needed information-processing skills.

3

INSTRUCTIONAL MODELS

Teaching is about learning. Teaching exists only for learning. And teachers have a wealth of choices to create diverse learning environments for students. There is no one best way of teaching, but only many approaches, many models, that enable each teacher to develop a personal theory for instruction.

Joyce and Weil (1972, p.3) define a *model* of teaching as "a pattern or plan which can be used to shape a curriculum or course, to select instructional materials, and to guide a teacher's actions." In this early conceptualization, Joyce and Weil proposed four families of models of teaching derived from the work of learning theorists like Skinner and Bruner, developmental psychologists such as Piaget and Hunt, counselors and therapists like Rogers and Maslow, philosophers such as James and Dewey, as well as from the practice of group dynamics, curriculum development, and experimental schools. These families of models reflect different views of human nature and the kinds of goals and environments that help human beings grow and develop and learn.

The four families represent differing views and sources of reality (much overlap exists).

♦ *Social Interaction Sources*—those that emphasize the relationships between the person and his or her culture (group investigation, jurisprudential approach, social inquiry and the laboratory/T-Group method);

+ *Information Processing Sources*—those that emphasize a learner's capacity for information processing (concept attainment, inductive thinking, inquiry training, science inquiry, advance organizer approach, intellectual development model);
+ *Personal and Humanistic Sources*—those oriented toward the individual person, personality development, and the personal construction of meaningful reality (nondirective teaching, classroom meeting model, Synectics/creativity development, awareness training);
+ *Behavior Modification Sources*—those derived from attempts to shape and reinforce human behavior (operant conditioning).

Joyce and Weil (1972) believe that the four families are the beginning points—not the recipes—for successful teaching. They advance a stimulating hypothesis:

> Teaching should be conceived as the creation of an environment composed of interdependent parts. Content, skills, instructional roles, social relationships, types of activities, physical facilities, and their use all add up to an environmental system whose parts interact with each other to constrain the behavior of all participants, teachers as well as students. Different combinations of these elements create different environments electing different educational outcomes. . . . Models for teaching are models for creating environments—they provide rough specifications which can be used to design and actualize learning environments.

Teachers and school administrators typically opt for models that support instructional outcomes or nurturing outcomes or both. The kinds of environments chosen determine the kinds of classrooms and schools that develop and the impact on learners.

The test of any model or theory is whether it can successfully guide practice. All good practice, in turn, is guided by theory. Theory is nothing more than knowledge based on research and experience that has proven to be generalizable to other situations.

Ornstein (1991) warns us that theory is not always easy to apply. Choosing the right methods for a given learning environment or content domain involves both experience and common sense. No matter how cogent a theory, it may not readily apply to every situation.

Teacher *style* is also an issue. Teaching styles are characteristic instructional behaviors reflective of teacher personality and educational philosophy (Keefe, 1989). Style is shown by what the teacher chooses to emphasize and how he or she responds to different learning situations. Ornstein (1991) argues that teachers integrate their theories and their chosen practices through their styles. Teachers have to be comfortable with what they do. They must come across to their students as comfortable with what they do. As a result, teaching style affects how teachers use and adapt research and theory in their teaching. Experienced teachers learn to choose among the available models and related practices to suit their own personal styles and the perceived needs of their students.

Research on teaching styles has focused on typologies of teaching behaviors. The most common distinction is directive versus nondirective or open style. (See Flanders, 1970; Bennett, 1976; Good, 1979.) Ramsey and Ransley (1986) discovered 10 elements of teaching style on a continuum from traditional to open. The open style was the least effective in relation to student outcomes. Schultz (1982) found that teachers attempted to create classroom learning environments in harmony with their teaching style *attitudes* (he did not look at their teaching *behaviors*). These and the findings of other researchers suggest that teaching style may be a significant factor influencing whether the learning environment is personalized or not.

More important to our current inquiry, however, is the work of recent years on paradigms of knowledge and instruction. Representative of this work is the monumental synthesis of Sylvia Farnham-Diggory of the University of Delaware. Farnham-Diggory (1994) proposes three core instructional paradigms (not four as Joyce and Weil suggested), and five types of knowledge that can be acquired within these frameworks. Farnham-Diggory defines the instructional models in terms of how novices are distinguished from and transformed into experts. Table 3.1 outlines these criteria for each of the three models in terms of behavior, development and apprenticeship. "Expert" in this synthesis means whatever level of competence a program establishes. "Novice" refers to whatever beginning level a program sets. "Transformation" implies whatever (inside the head) turns the novice into the expert.

TABLE 3.1. INSTRUCTIONAL MODEL CRITERIA

Instructional Paradigm	Expert-Novice Distinction	Key Mechanism of Transformation
Behavior	Quantitative differences on the same scale(s)	Incrementation
Development	Differences in qualitative models (personal beliefs)	Perturbation
Apprenticeship	Sociological differences in the culture of practice	Acculturation

PARADIGMS OF INSTRUCTION

THE BEHAVIOR MODEL

In the behavior model, novices and experts are rated on the same scale(s), with the former low and the latter high. The novice becomes an expert by improving on the scale, by gaining something ("Incrementation"). The result is a *quantitative* shift. This model goes back to Edward Thorndike (1918) who had a rule for almost everything. He used to say that anything that exists, exists in some amount. He stressed that what is taught and learned can be measured. Contemporary instructional theory and practice are still influenced by his three main laws of learning:

(1) *Law of Exercise* (repetition strengthens the connections between stimulus and response); (2) *Law of Effect* (connections that are satisfying will be strengthened; those that are annoying will be weakened); and (3) *Law of Readiness* (learner preparation and interest determines at least in part what satisfies or annoys).

Farnham-Diggory (1994) cites an example of this model in remedial reading called Intensive Literacy in which students are taught letter-to-sound correspondences (called "phonograms") and various rules about English words. Students learn about 70 phonograms and 30 rules for spelling and reading words. They are tested regularly on word lists in the process of building a personal wordbook based on the rules.

THE DEVELOPMENT MODEL

Novices and experts are differentiated by their personal theories and explanations of life events and experiences. The novice often has primitive or naive views of events that experts thoroughly understand. Instruction proceeds by questioning and challenging the novice's naive mental models in order to confound them and to encourage revision ("perturbation"). The result is a *qualitative* shift.

Many of Piaget's findings illustrate this paradigm. In the stage of intuitive thought (ages 4 to 7), a child presented with two jars of equal capacity and contents, one narrow and the other wide, will judge that the narrow jar has more water than the wide one because the levels rise higher in the former. Farnham-Diggory (1994) cites Deborah Smith's "Shadows" curriculum to illustrate how students' mental models can change. First and second grade science students believe (in line with Piaget's findings) that their shadows project from the front of their bodies, exist in the dark, and are like mirror images. Smith designed a series of projects using shadows that countered these beliefs. The children then constructed new theories—that shadows come from light that is blocked and that mirror images come from bouncing, not blocked light.

THE APPRENTICESHIP MODEL

In this model, novices and experts live in different cultures. The novice becomes an expert through a process of "acculturation" into the world of the expert. Actual participation is required because much of the knowledge to be learned is implied and informal (tacit) and varies with the context.

Almost any apprenticeship situation illustrates this mode of instruction. (It is almost initiation.) Apprentice teachers, for example, have usually read widely about the science and craft of teaching, but typically have little idea how to mount the processes of planning, materials selection, class management, instruction, and assessment without practice teaching and mentoring by experienced colleagues. Much of this knowledge has to be experienced and application varies widely from school to school.

INSTRUCTION AND LEARNING

Information Processing and cognitive processes are inherent to all three instructional models. Nothing can be taught without cognitive processes and knowledge bases. Cognitive procedures provide the basis for all instruction, regardless of the model. Cognition per se, however, does not constitute a separate instructional model. Farnham-Diggory (1994) postulates that five types of knowledge operate within each of the three instructional models. These five types flow from five different paradigms of learning developed by experimental psychologists from the 1930s through the 1960s. Each of the knowledge types calls for different kinds of instruction. Since the types are studied and acquired in different ways, students need appropriate learning conditions and environments to acquire them.

TYPES OF KNOWLEDGE

DECLARATIVE KNOWLEDGE

Most knowledge that is taught in typical schools is declarative in format. It is transmitted in *symbols*, usually words, but also in mathematical notation or in some other symbolic language.

It is "declared" through lectures, books, conversation, sign language, computers, etc. If, for instance, I explain that I am a teacher who studied at a particular university and have taught a given subject for a certain number of years, I have "declared" the *facts* of my educational resume.

PROCEDURAL KNOWLEDGE

Procedural knowledge is about *skills*. Beyond the talking and reading and gesturing, the learner must be able to *do* something—to demonstrate skills in various sequences of actions. Talking about teaching is not the same as doing it. A monumental body of information exits on skill learning in almost every conceivable field. Whatever the body of knowledge, skill development passes through three phases: (1) analysis (i.e., watching others); (2) practice to automaticity (e.g., practice teaching); (3) attention management (i.e., skilled performance). The latter phase is called "concentration" by athletes and performers and assumes that no analysis is needed for the (automatic) behavior.

CONCEPTUAL KNOWLEDGE

Conceptual knowledge is either *categorical* or *schematic*. Categories are generic attributes. For example, I know about teaching in a general way and can describe its characteristics. Schemata add spatial and temporal attributes. I know the layout of classrooms and different teaching environments and I have several "scripts" in my mind for teaching under these varying conditions.

Conceptual knowledge is acquired through repeated experiences in extracting commonalities. A concept is the knowledge of a commonality derived from personal experience. Each teacher, for example, has constructed his or her concepts of teaching from personal experiences.

ANALOGICAL KNOWLEDGE

Analogies are specific matches between reality and a person's mind. Analogical knowledge is sometimes called *imagery*. Images may come from a single impression or many impressions of something in reality, but a *pattern* remains. Individuals asked to recall the face of a mugger usually have no problem picking out the individual from a police book. I remember my high school and my favorite classrooms quite readily even though I have not seen them for many years. Strong analogical knowledge seems to leave a kind of imprint on long-term memory.

LOGICAL KNOWLEDGE

Logical knowledge is an individual's *mental model* of something in reality. The model may or may not be accurate by some objective standard, but it is always accompanied by a strong *conviction*, what Piaget called a "feeling of necessity." Research may indicate that certain approaches to instruction and learning are more successful than my own approach, but I believe in my approach. It is more compelling to me. Logical knowledge arises from one's own reasoning, not from facts or skill or even categorical or schematic knowledge. (Much of our information about logical knowledge comes from research on problem solving.)

METAKNOWLEDGE AND METACOGNITION

It is important here to distinguish types of knowledge from the knowledge about knowing. Metaknowledge is knowing you know something, whether declarative, procedural, conceptual, analogical, or logical. Even young children have this capability. Metacognition is the ability to control one's cognition by monitoring and analyzing one's current learning and by selecting appropriate strategies to remediate difficulties. Early psychologists called some of these skills "cognitive controls" (see Chapter 2). Sternberg calls them "metacomponents." Skilled students constantly check their learning processes, look for clues and procedures to apply them to the learning at-hand, and strive to construct efficient working memory programs. (Learning *strategies* are acquisition *tasks* in a given subject domain. More about these in Chapter 5.)

INSTRUCTIONAL PRACTICE

All five kinds of knowledge can be learned within any of the three main instructional models—behavioral, developmental or apprenticeship—but different paradigms do demand different knowledge acquisition strategies.

The paradigm most commonly found in American schools was derived from the behavioral research of Edward Thorndike and B.F. Skinner, and the learning hierarchies of Robert Gagne and Benjamin Bloom. The behavioral tradition stresses assessment (everything must be measured), behavioral objectives, hierarchical task analysis (scope and sequence), explicit teaching/direct instruction, and reinforcement strategies (a structure of rewards and punishments). Various attempts have been made to change this dominant paradigm, but with little success. "Back-to-basics" countermovements have always forced schools back each time to instructional practices based on early 20th century behavioral psychology.

Cognitive approaches to psychology became influential in the 1950s and began to assert some sway over instructional practice in the 1970s. Cognitive *developmental* models emphasize the complexity and gestalt of learning whereas behavioral models stress breaking everything down into units. Developmental models utilize performance evaluation such as student portfolios and exhibitions which require expert judgment on the part of evaluators; behavioral models favor paper-and-pencil tests. Developmental models emphasize holistic learning environments with long-term projects. Behavioral models tend to stress individual work on (largely) abstract academic tasks. The heart and soul of the developmental model is a *learning environment* designed to involve students and teachers in a total learning experience.

Cognitive *apprenticeship* models marry the principles of John Dewey's laboratory school and contemporary computer learning environments with the craft apprenticeship. Experts and novices collaborate on common projects. The experts (teachers) show the novices (students) what to do. Traditional schooling, in fact, is nothing more than a behaviorist apprenticeship that replaced the craft apprenticeships of the 18th and early 19th centuries.

In a cognitive apprenticeship, the experts (teachers, parents, mentors, peer tutors) work together with apprentices (the students) on important projects that have meaning and value in the real world. The experts share their thinking and decision-making processes, admitting mistakes, beginning again, assisting and mentoring their charges who attempt to follow as best they can. Assessment involves talking about what has been done. Teachers ask students to describe what they have been doing and why they are doing it. The tasks gradually become longer and more complex, with the experts helping the apprentices to grasp any general principles involved in their thinking and doing. Eventually the apprentices are given and accept responsibility for new tasks and projects. With some supervision, they are on their own.

Many high school science labs and industrial arts classes have used the apprenticeship approach over the years. Electronic, computer graphic and technology labs increasingly employ the approach. The major difference between craft and cognitive approaches is that strategies and methods can usually be demonstrated in a craft, whereas they must be described in words in a cognitive apprenticeship. The Jordanhill College of Education in Glasgow, Scotland, for example, has developed an apprenticeship method called *topic study* that begins each unit with a story, proposes problem-solving issues, and incorporates research, experiments, art and media projects, writing, etc. Students are taught how to use computers as tools—for accessing data, simulation, designing, and editing—just as adults use them (see Farnham-Diggory, 1992, pp. 580–608).

These cognitive (developmental and apprenticeship) approaches have several features in common:

1. Emphasis is on integrated models of learning reflecting what cognitive scientists are now hypothesizing about the mental processes involved in learning. The first task of the teacher is to develop a personal mental model of teaching based on contemporary cognitive science.

   - Cognitive models are based on what competent adults do on target tasks.

Teachers consult experts in the various domains (reading, writing, music, etc.) to be able to model their performance in the tasks and skills of the domain.

- All five types of knowledge are important—declarative, procedural, conceptual, analogical and logical. Teachers establish learning environments that facilitate students in acquiring the appropriate knowledge for the task or project

- Long-term memory thrives on long-term and integrated activities. Teachers use long-term projects in which students have many opportunities for shared learning.

- New knowledge is acquired by incorporating it into the network of long-term memory. Teachers start with what students know and help them build working memory programs that establish goals, attend to relevant data, retrieve goal-relevant knowledge from long-term memory, and learn to monitor the process and its progress.

2. Cognitive assessment is holistic, complex and based on real-world performance. Information processing is involved in all performance, including assessment. *Doing something*, in many instances, is more important than being able to describe it.

- Assessing competence on complex tasks and skills calls for looking at the *performance* itself, not the isolated parts. Judging total performance has long been the standard in the arts and in athletics. Judging such performance requires that teachers be trained in the standards for complex human thinking and learning.

- Progress on long-term projects is ongoing and progress reporting must be longitudinal. Students themselves and teachers keep track using computer programs and summary reports.

- Diagnostic information is important to students, teachers and parents if student information processing difficulties are to be corrected and coaching is to be successful. Diagnosis can be facilitated by advisement arrangements (teacher adviser, adviser/advisee), cognitive style assessment, teacher observation of students, careful anecdotal record keeping, etc.

- The results of long-range projects are best displayed in student portfolios and in various exhibitions of student work.

3. Traditional schooling reflects outmoded factory models of organization and behavioral models of apprenticeship. "Most problems of motivation and classroom control are artifacts of this rather peculiar learning environment. The way to address these problems, then, is to change the environment that gives rise to them" (Farnham-Diggory, 1992, p. 576). The key to solving most social and motivational problems in today's schools is to alter the learning environments that cause or occasion them. As systems theory suggests, the problem is not with the people, but with the structure itself. Cognitive science proposes that new learning environments be designed that better support student motivation, information processing and task success.

AN INSTRUCTIONAL SYSTEM

All human learning is personal. No one can learn for anyone else. Neither can anybody teach anyone anything unless they want to learn it. Each learner learns for himself. In this sense at least, all learning is and always has been an individual activity. Burns (1974) defines learning as "a process (p) which occurs over some period of time (t) and always involves an individual learner (L) achieving some objective (O)." In traditional classroom instruction, all learners are treated as constants (c) with both time and process as constants. Only achievement is allowed to vary. Those who need more time or different treatment learn less and receive lower grades. (See Figure 3.1).

FIGURE 3.1. TRADITIONAL VS. PERSONALIZED LEARNING
(Adapted from Richard Burns, 1974)

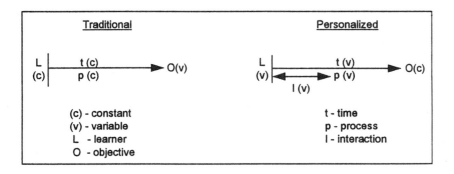

In personalized learning, the learner is viewed as unique and hence variable (v). Time and process are allowed to vary so that each learner can achieve what needs to be learned. But these components do not tell the whole story, because personalized learning also involves interaction (I)—between the learner and teachers, computers, other resources. Of course, neither time nor process are allowed to vary unrestrictedly in real school settings. Some restriction always exists on the amount of time a learner can (or will be allowed to) take to complete a given objective. We surely do not want 22- or 23-year-olds still in high school. Neither is the process as variable as it might be, even in the most personalized settings. But interaction is the key to personalization.

At root, the measure of personalization is the *quality* of interaction between learner and process. The function of the teacher in personalization is to optimize the interaction.

A personalized instructional system utilizes the strategies of diagnosis, prescription, instruction, and evaluation (DPIE). Personalization is any effort on the part of a school to take into account individual student characteristics and effective instructional practices in organizing the learning environment. It can support behavioral, developmental, or apprenticeship instructional models. The teacher committed to personalization helps students put together a personal learning plan, assists in diagnosing cognitive strengths and weaknesses, provides cognitive skill training as needed, adapts instruction to learner needs and interests and monitors progress. The teacher is coach, adviser, and mentor. The teacher is no longer so much an educational broadcaster as an academic troubleshooter and cognitive facilitator.

Figure 3.2 presents a systems model of personalized diagnosis, prescription, instruction, and evaluation. Personalized education begins with the learner and builds the learning environment on learner needs and interests. The foundation of a personalized approach is *diagnosis*—the assessment of individual learner characteristics, knowledge and skills. Teachers spend substantial time on the three important aspects of the diagnostic process: (1) finding out where students are in the learning process; (2) observing student progress in learning (progress checks); and (3) prescribing or suggesting learning procedures and resources that enable the student to learn at an optimal rate for his capabilities and aptitudes (learning style).

Glasser and Nitko (1971) characterize diagnosis as a decision about appropriate teaching techniques for a given student. Besel (1973) compares instructional diagnosis to medical treatment and electronic troubleshooting but points out that the analogy breaks down when placement (not remediation) is the focus.

Wong and Raulerson (1974) talk of "pre-assessment" as the first phase of a systems plan for instruction. The ideal way to

FIGURE 3.2. MODEL OF PERSONALIZED EDUCATION
(Keefe, 1995)

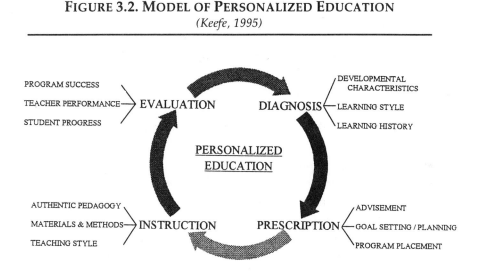

find out whether students possess a particular knowledge or skill, of course, is to ask them to perform. Lacking direct feedback, however, some other form of assessment can give indication of what a student still needs to learn.

Prescription deals with decisions about placement and process. Both are aspects of appropriate planning. Instruction and evaluation have many meanings depending on the context. We will define these terms operationally within the DPIE cycle. The cycle has four stages and 12 steps (Keefe, 1989):

1. *Diagnosis is concerned with student traits, learning skills, and the nature of the learning environment. It encompasses student developmental characteristics, learning history (Bloom's term for acquired knowledge and skills), and cognitive/learning style. Analysis of student learning traits is the most basic DPIE element. Teachers determine the current readiness, cognitive skills, strengths, and weaknesses of each student by observation or assessment.*

- Developmental characteristics are stages in individual maturation when various capacities for learned behavior appear (e.g., visual perception, language pronunciation, cognitive thinking skills). These characteristics tell us *when* a student is developmentally ready to learn something. They describe physiological readiness for learning.

- Learning styles are characteristic cognitive, affective and physiological behaviors that serve as relatively stable indicators of how students perceive, interact with, and respond to the learning environment (Keefe, 1979). The cognitive behaviors are the foundation. Learning style basically tells us *how* a student learns and prefers to learn. (See Fig. 3.3.)

FIGURE 3.3. TYPOLOGY OF LEARNING STYLES

Cognitive Styles Are Information Processing Habits related to:	*Affective Styles Are Motivational Processes* responsible for:	*Physiological Styles Are Biologically-Based Responses*:
• Perceiving	• Arousing Attention	• Gender-related Learning Differences
• Thinking	• Directing Activity	• Health-related Behavior
• Problem-solving	• Sustaining Interest	• Reactions to the Environment
• Remembering		

- Learning history describes *what* a student knows and feels at a given point in his/her learning career—the knowledge, the skills, and the attitudes a student possesses at the beginning of a new learning experience. These levels may be assessed by observation, performance tests, curriculum-referenced tests, attitude inventories, etc.

2. *Prescription is concerned with advisement, goal setting, program planning and placement, and appropriate processes for learning. Teachers determine appropriate instructional objectives and activities, as well as grouping and scheduling alternatives.*

   - Advisement is a process that brings the student continuously into contact with persons, places, and actions which facilitate development of the student's talents and interests. The teacher advisor (TA) is the key person in this process. Each student has an adult advisor.

   - Goal setting and program planning begin with a diagnostic profile developed for each student from available diagnostic data. Program planning utilizes the diagnostic profile to set personal and career goals. Students need both multiyear and 1-year plans. The multiyear plan establishes long-range educational direction based on discussion among parents, teacher-adviser and the student. A 1-year plan focuses on the student's program and projects for the current year.

   - Program placement involves scheduling the student in appropriate learning activities; materials and methods must address student skill needs and learning styles. The

school schedule provides for both flexibility
and adequate structure.

3. *Instruction embraces teacher styles, study skills and
    authentic pedagogy. Teachers are involved in structur-
    ing the learning environment, communicating
    information, monitoring and responding to student
    needs, encouraging students in the appropriate use
    of time, etc.*

    • Teaching styles are characteristic instruc-
      tional behaviors reflective of teacher
      personality and educational philosophy
      (Keefe, 1989). Different teaching styles
      produce different learning environments.
      The most successful teachers adapt their
      styles.

    • Variable materials and methods are
      necessary because students have different
      styles and skill levels. Teaching focuses
      on the appropriate cognitive processes, the
      learning environment, the content to be
      studied, and the available resources. It
      involves structuring, interacting, facilitat-
      ing, evaluating. Methodologies can range
      from computer-based learning, learning
      guides and group activities to experiential
      learning, project work, etc.

    • Authentic pedagogy and other proven
      instructional strategies are used to enhance
      student success in learning. Student
      progress is monitored and students are
      regularly given feedback on the quality
      of their study habits and schoolwork.

4. *Evaluation encompasses student progress reporting,
    teacher supervision, and program evaluation.*

    • Student achievement is analyzed and
      reported in terms of personal growth or
      performance criteria rather than by group

standing. Grades, if given, are assigned on an absolute basis certifying what a student has or has not learned. The student competes with self and collaborates with classmates.

- Teacher supervision is based on peer appraisal and mutually agreed upon goals. Teachers work in collaborative teams so individual performance appraisal is less meaningful.

- The total school curriculum is evaluated in terms of whether district and school philosophy, goals, and objectives are being met.

A feedback loop using data from student performance, teacher supervision, and program evaluation allows for (a) continuation, modification, or termination of any program, (b) continuing diagnosis of student skills and needs, and (c) repetition of the entire DPIE cycle.

DPIE takes place in supervised study, in small groups, and in media and resource centers—teachers working with students who exhibit similar needs and/or interests. Some DPIE does occur on a one-to-one basis, but this option is not very efficient in the use of staff time. More often, teachers mentor students who "cluster" at the same point in the curriculum or on the same project.

A personalized instructional system can support many learning paradigms and methodologies. It is particularly helpful in an apprenticeship model, and in one that stresses student growth in life-related knowledge and skills. It supports an integrated vision of learning and school improvement. It is for this reason that we have recently incorporated authentic pedagogy into the system. Chapter 4 explores the standards and characteristics of authentic learning, authentic assessment and authentic student performance.

ACTION STEPS

♦ Evaluate the general instructional organization of your school. Is it behavioral, developmental or an apprenticeship? Is it an active or a passive learning environment? Do you see ways that it might be altered for the better?

♦ Of the five types of knowledge, which type(s) does your school emphasize in typical instruction? If primarily declarative, is there an application component? If primarily procedural or conceptual, what skills and working programs or scripts predominate? If analogical or logical, how are students encouraged to develop imagery and mental models?

♦ Can you envision your school operating as a series of cognitive apprenticeships? Are your teachers sufficiently open minded and risk oriented to try such an approach? Prepare a plan that encourages teachers to support students in long-term and collaborative projects in which the goal is the production of *new* knowledge—a product or performance or skill.

♦ Personalization requires a flexible learning environment. With your school staff, develop a strategic plan (3–5 years) to introduce personalized education to your school. Focus initially on learning style assessment, teacher advisement and developing personal educational plans for each student.

4

AUTHENTIC PEDAGOGY

The essence of the contemporary cognitive movement can be grasped most readily in the instructional model called the apprenticeship. As we saw in Chapter 3, the thrust of this paradigm is a process of "acculturation" whereby the novice learner increasingly participates in the world of the expert. The apprentice works with adult mentors to acquire the kinds of knowledge, skills, and attitudes that enable the skilled expert to perform successfully in the adult world.

The apprenticeship model fits well with a constructivist view of learning. In constructivism, the learner actively makes personal meaning by confronting the real-world implications of any new information, skill, or attitude to be processed. Learning is an active process requiring participation and interaction with mentors, materials, and meaning. These are the "3Ms" of active learning which directly challenge the assumptions of traditional, largely passive, learning and instruction. Learners are continually striving to "make sense" of whatever they meet in any learning situation. Student's learning is strongly influenced by their previous knowledge, the nature of their current learning environment, and their patterns of information processing and self-monitoring.

Teachers are mentors and coaches in a constructivist system. Newmann, Marks and Gamoran (1995) outline several principles of active instructional practice from the literature.

♦ Teachers must know and actively use the prior knowledge that students bring to the teaching-learning situation. Students are inclined to accept new information that explores and extends what they already know. This is an argument both for teachers starting instruction where they find students in their pursuit of knowledge (not on the first page of a textbook) and for the careful diagnosis of students' developmental level, learning style, and learning history called for in personalized learning (see Chapter 3).

♦ Teachers must reject rote learning and superficial coverage in favor of higher-order thinking and in-depth understanding. Traditional classroom approaches tend to encourage the former. (TQM tells us that the *structure* is the issue.) Developmental and apprenticeship approaches facilitate the latter.

♦ Teachers must encourage the active making of meaning by offering students many opportunities to express themselves—in speaking, in writing, in music, art, drama, and sports, in complex projects that engage all these modes of expression. Students must actually *process* information to make it their own in long-term memory.

♦ Teachers must serve as mentors, facilitators, guides and coaches in a "cognitive apprenticeship." The times when teachers could simply read their notes to classrooms of bored students are not only long passed, but simply irrelevant to contemporary learning and instruction. Active learning requires active learners *and* teachers.

♦ Teachers and students must collaborate, exhibit mutual trust, and share high expectations for success. The apprenticeship model is a collaboration built on respect, cooperation, and commitment to a common goal—the preparation of the learner for a meaningful adult life.

AUTHENTIC ACHIEVEMENT

Authentic Pedagogy focuses on the kind of mastery found in successful adults. Traditional schooling has been concerned with structured classrooms, authoritative teachers, passive learners, content coverage, Carnegie units and semester credits, competitive grades, and standardized achievement test scores. *Authentic* human achievement, on the other hand, is concerned with what is significant, worthwhile, and meaningful in the lives of successful adults from all walks of life—artists, business people, electricians, lawyers, plumbers, scientists, teachers, technicians, etc. Authentic *academic* achievement, then, should concern itself with accomplishments that are significant, worthwhile, and meaningful for students preparing for adulthood.

The Center on Organization and Restructuring of Schools (CORS) at the University of Wisconsin-Madison devoted 5 years of research to the formulation and study of criteria and standards for authentic academic achievement, authentic instruction, authentic assessment tasks, and authentic performance (Newmann, Marks, & Gamoran 1995; Newmann, Secada, & Wehlage, 1995; Newmann & Wehlage, 1995). The center characterizes academic achievement in terms of three criteria: (1) construction of knowledge, (2) disciplined inquiry, and (3) value beyond school.

CONSTRUCTION OF KNOWLEDGE

Traditional education generally asks students to *reproduce* knowledge, to label and identify things, rather than to *produce* something. But adults in many fields must actually produce something—new knowledge and processes and products. Adult professionals or technicians or craftsmen build on prior knowledge developed by others to generate oral or written discourse (speeches, compositions), to build or fix things (art, architecture, manufacture), and to produce various performances (music, drama, sports). Students, of course, are not expected to produce at the level of adults, but the process of construction is much the same. Students must build on prior knowledge. They must organize, analyze, synthesize, explain, or evaluate information.

They must perfect their skills under expert tutelage. In short, they must organize information and consider alternatives.

Conventional schooling emphasizes identification, recognition and recall. The important tasks involve memorizing words or formulas, recognizing concepts like nouns and verbs or the elements of the periodic table, recalling the names of authors and their works, or historical figures and their events and dates. Authentic achievement asks students to produce real compositions and presentations, to engage in thoughtful conversation or discussion, to mount significant projects, to use technology, to repair automobiles and other things, to perform in plays and musicals and games. Here we are not talking about a few highly talented students, but *all* students. Authentic achievement involves all students in *active* and *meaningful* learning.

DISCIPLINED INQUIRY

Academic achievement focuses on fields of knowledge that have specific facts, vocabulary, concepts, and theories. Disciplined inquiry is concerned with the use of a prior knowledge base, in-depth understanding of an issue or problem, and complex forms of communication to perform the work and to convey it to others.

Most work in traditional schools entails the transfer of existing knowledge to students. This is just the starting point for authentic achievement. Disciplined inquiry demands that learners use prior knowledge to understand new problems, not simply to assemble a catalog of facts. Disciplined inquiry stresses the probing function of working memory that ties new information to that already stored in long-term memory. The goal is in-depth understanding rather than wide content coverage. Students explore the ideas, relationships and inconsistencies of limited issues and problems to move beyond superficial awareness. Then, as do engineers and journalists and many other skilled adults, they express their findings and conclusions in real forms of communication (verbal, visual, symbolic) rather than in the short-answer tests of traditional schooling.

VALUE BEYOND SCHOOL

Authentic academic achievement always has personal or utilitarian or aesthetic value beyond school grades or honor rolls or college scholarships. Successful adults write, or speak, or build, or create something, with a practical purpose, not just to affirm their competence. They want their ideas and products to be used by others, to have an impact on others. The tasks of traditional schooling often have little value apart from ranking students or classifying them for other similar tasks. Authentic student achievement has value beyond simply measuring success in school.

AUTHENTIC ACHIEVEMENT AS FACILITATOR

Not all three criteria of authentic achievement may be present in every instructional setting, but all three are important. A work of literature or a math problem may be intellectually stimulating and require in-depth understanding and yet have little relevance for the real-world of the student, either now or later. Repetitive practice and seatwork may be necessary to build a knowledge base, but will likely fall short on authenticity. (Even memory work may become more authentic with the use of interactive computer programs and more interesting content.) The important issue here is that authentic academic achievement facilitates both engagement and transfer (Newmann, Secada, & Wehlage, 1995). Authentic tasks are more likely to motivate students to undertake and continue the work that real learning requires. Students are more likely to use the real-world knowledge and the skills of higher-order thinking and problem-solving that authentic achievement engenders.

AUTHENTIC INSTRUCTION

Authentic academic achievement demands an instructional process that supports the three criteria of intellectual quality discussed in the previous section. Many contemporary school restructuring practices can promote active and meaningful learning, but small group discussions, experiential learning, and hands-on projects do not in themselves ensure authenticity. These activities may be as sterile as nonstop lecturing if they do not encourage construction of knowledge, in-depth understanding, and value beyond school.

Several indicators or standards serve to affirm that instruction in a school is authentic (Newmann, Secada & Wehlage, 1995).

1. *Authentic instruction is characterized by higher-order thinking.* Higher-order thinking involves learners in constructing knowledge, in analyzing, synthesizing, and evaluating, in integrating, assimilating, differentiating, and associating information for storage in and recall from long-term memory. The construction of knowledge requires both good cognitive control—the ability to manage the thinking process—and use of problem-solving skills.

The CORS study in 24 restructured schools offers some insightful examples of authentic instruction. The teacher in one eighth grade social studies class, for example, asked students to reflect on the impact that worker layoffs might have on the community. The teacher initiated the inquiry by defining terms ("layoff," "fringe benefits," "unemployment compensation," etc.) and presenting data on the local community and two other similar communities with different business conditions. Students formed small groups to consider the question, "What generalizations can you state about each of the local economies?" After discussion, the students developed this generalization: Layoffs mean the loss of salaries and less spending in the community. They also developed hypotheses about local business failures and about healthcare impact.

This instruction scores well on higher-order thinking. All students actively participated in constructing knowledge through analyzing information, making comparisons and generating hypotheses about the issue.

2. *Authentic instruction is characterized by deep knowledge.* Authentic thinking focuses in-depth on the central ideas and concepts of a topic in order

to examine relationships and to generate complex understandings. Authentic instruction stimulates students to consider their prior knowledge and to explore connections with the ideas under consideration.

The CORS study describes a fifth grade social studies class that compared North American Indian tribes on the basis of culture. The teacher began by defining culture and its major components (housing, clothing, food gathering, and distinctive customs). Students were divided into two small groups and asked to prepare reports comparing two tribes on these cultural subcategories. Students used library materials while the teacher circulated, asked questions, and challenged students to think about the meaning of culture. Student reports emphasized similarities and differences and focused on distinctive customs like the Northwest Coast American Indians' "potlatch" celebration.

This instruction rated high on deep knowledge because almost all students demonstrated significant understanding of how Indian cultures were similar or different.

3. *Authentic instruction features substantive conversation.* Students and teachers engage in extended and reflective conversations to build a shared understanding of subject content. Classroom discourse is thoughtful and interactive.

The CORS study cites a high school mathematics/physics class where students and teacher collaborated in the design of an amusement park ride. A previous class had designed a free-fall ride that was 125 meters high. The teacher asked class members to consider the design characteristics of the ride, the actual speed the ride would be traveling at the bottom of the fall, and whether it would be safe. At first, the students thought the ride would be safe, but reconsidered after the teacher challenged them to look at the specifications of an (actual) nearby park ride that was only 14 meters high and yet very fast. The students and the teacher discussed the various relationships among the concepts—the distance the ride fell, the velocity and acceleration, and the amount of time the ride took to stop. They decided that the 125-meter ride was probably unsafe. What was even more significant, however, was that the students and their teacher spent the entire 2-hour class talking about the relevance of such ideas as Newton's second law of physics ($F = m*a$), the real import of acceleration and deceleration, the effect of ride curves on deceleration, and even whether the maneuvers of the Starship Enterprise (on the television program "Star Trek") were feasible (they weren't).

This activity scored high on substantive conversation because it created sustained, shared, and thoughtful conversation for virtually all participants.

4. *Authentic instruction creates connections to the world beyond the classroom.* Instruction connects the knowledge generated in school with real world topics of personal or public concern. Teachers help students to see the relationships between school learning and issues and problems of the outside world.

The CORS study describes a fourth grade mathematics class in which students were asked to figure the costs of managing a household on no more than $2,000 per month. The teacher provided categories for the analyses (i.e., rent, groceries, utilities) and real-world references for computing costs (a real estate guide, grocery receipts, telephone, gas, and water bills). Students carefully studied the costs and made some hard choices like renting a cheaper apartment to stay within budget.

This instruction was high on real-world connections because students were forced to come to grips with decisions in life beyond school.

Not all these examples rate strongly on all four indicators of authentic instruction. The "free-fall ride" example from the mathematics/physics class comes closest. The social studies "layoff" example is high in higher-order thinking and substantive conversation, but lower in depth of knowledge and connections to the real world (it was fairly abstract). One key to improving this kind of instruction lies with the assessment tasks that teachers employ to evaluate student learning.

AUTHENTIC ASSESSMENT

Traditional schooling relies heavily on simple paper-and-pencil, multiple-choice tests to verify student learning. Students are asked to memorize and recall discrete bits of information from textbooks or teacher lectures. Even many essay examinations require this kind of intellectual regurgitation. The nature of the assessment tasks that teachers use sends a clear message about the kind of schoolwork that is valued. Traditional tests signal that memorization and simple recall are valuable. If students are to prize high quality intellectual work, however, assessment tasks must signal that knowledge construction (not recall), disciplined inquiry, and real-world products are highly valued. The CORS School Restructuring Study (Newmann & Wehlage, 1995) collected many examples of assessment tasks from teachers in elementary, middle, and senior high schools. These activities ranged from typical short-answer tests and essays to projects and reports. Although the CORS study considered only written assessment tasks because of time and staffing limitations, both written and nonwritten performance can be authentic (*cf.* Herman, Aschbacher, & Winters, 1992). Seven standards emerged from the study that reflect the three general characteristics of authentic human achievement.

CONSTRUCTION OF KNOWLEDGE

An assessment task that calls for the construction of knowledge requires students to *organize information and to consider alternatives*.

- ♦ *Organization of information* demands that students interpret, evaluate and utilize information in a systematic way. For example, fourth and fifth grade students in the CORS study had to use measurement and fractions to design and draw a diagram of a bookcase and to show how the wood would be cut. Eighth grade students were asked to write a social studies report comparing American immigration issues in the past and present. Students had to gather and organize information, make comparisons and draw generalization about key immigration groups, causes of immigration and national policies, and discuss the implications for the present.

♦ *Consideration of alternatives* demands that students be open to differing perspectives, strategies and solutions. For example, eighth grade students in the CORS study were engaged in building a set of regular polyhedrons (three-dimensional figures with straight-line edges like a pyramid or box). Students had to consider alternative shapes that would fit the definition of a regular polyhedron, how to build them, and why the possibilities were limited.

Other eighth graders completed a history report in which they acted as advisers to President Richard Nixon after the 1968 election. They were required to discuss the pros and cons of United States involvement in Vietnam, cite statistics and other background information, anticipate points of disagreement and less defensible views, and make a final recommendation.

DISCIPLINED INQUIRY

Assessment tasks reflecting disciplined inquiry require the *understanding of disciplinary content* (subject matter), the use of *appropriate methods of inquiry* for the discipline, and *elaborated written communication*.

♦ *Understanding disciplinary content* focuses on the concepts, theories and paradigms of an academic or professional discipline. Fifth graders in the CORS study drew geometric designs of their own making and wrote BASIC (software) programs that would replicate the designs. Writing the programs required students to create algorithms for their designs.

CORS high school history students compared Franklin D. Roosevelt's "Three Rs" (Relief, Recovery, Reform) of the 1930s Depression with Bill Clinton's "jumpstart" to stimulate economic recovery in the 1990s. They compared and contrasted 1930s economic assumptions and theory with those of the present, exhibiting an understanding of the effect of government actions and market forces on employment, earnings, and investments.

+ *Appropriate process* implies the methods, research, and characteristic language of a discipline. Fifth graders in the CORS sample had to explain the relationships between the number of teeth in a gear and the number of turns another gear with a different number of teeth would take when the first gear completed a turn. Students had to search for patterns and create generalizations for writing about ratios and proportions in new situations.

A CORS fourth-fifth grade social studies class engaged in a project in urban geography that involved a year-long study of their community. Working in small groups, they selected a neighborhood, inventoried its current features, facilities, transportation patterns and traffic flow, and identified any special problems. Students weighed various plans for neighborhood improvement, eventually deciding on one, drawing it up, and explaining its merits.

+ *Elaborated written communication* involves writing about one's understandings, explanations, findings, and conclusions. Middle school students in the CORS study wrote essays on the 1992 presidential election. Among the six topics they could choose was writing an editorial to persuade voters to vote, using examples from history to show the importance of the vote. Essays were evaluated on criteria that required students to include facts from class, to go beyond what was learned in class to other sources of information, and to support opinion with reasons. Students "elaborated" on the facts to develop persuasive arguments.

VALUE BEYOND SCHOOL

Assessment tasks meet this standard when they speak to a *problem* and an *audience* outside the classroom. Students must address a real-world problem and communicate their conclusions to an audience beyond the school.

- A problem addresses a *real-world issue* when it is or can be connected to the world beyond school. CORS high school students were presented with this geometry task:

  Design packaging that will hold 576 cans of Campbell's Tomato Soup (net weight, 10¾ oz.) or packaging that will hold 144 boxes of Kellogg's Rice Krispies (net weight, 19 oz.). Use and list each individual package's real measurements; create scale drawings of fronts, top, and side perspectives; show the unfolded boxes/container in a scale drawing; build a proportional, three-dimensional model.

  Students wrote a short summary of how they completed the project, made an oral presentation, and answered the question, "How does space involve geometry?"

- An assessment task addresses an *audience beyond school* when students communicate their knowledge, design a product, present a performance or take an action that relates to a real-world audience. CORS fourth graders studying ecology wrote letters to their state assembly representatives or senators expressing their opinions on what to do about eagles threatened along the Mississippi River. Students had to meet various criteria about letter organization, format, punctuation, spelling, and communication of ideas.

This final assessment task actually meets several of the standards for authentic assessment, including organizing information, considering alternatives, and addressing a problem in an elaborated way to an actual audience beyond the school. It should be clear from this and the other examples that the quality of instruction is directly affected by the authenticity of the assessment tasks that teachers select. It remains for us to discuss the nature of student performance—the success or proficiency that students achieve as a result of authentic pedagogy.

AUTHENTIC STUDENT PERFORMANCE

How can we know that student academic achievement resulting from authentic instruction and assessment is actually high quality performance? How can we rate the proficiency and success of student achievement? The CORS study proposes three criteria relating to knowledge construction and disciplined inquiry: (1) the quality of student analysis; (2) student use of disciplinary concepts; and (3) student use of elaborated written communication. The CORS research was limited to written performance, but we could readily expect similar criteria for non-written performances like debates, computer designs or dramas.

The criterion for *knowledge construction* is the quality of *analysis* that a student brings to an academic task. Analysis is the capability to separate a concept or product into its component parts in order to determine its structure. Analysis examines and interprets. High quality analysis is characterized by focus, careful classification of parts, and an understanding of the structure revealed. (Analytic skill is a key cognitive control that can be improved by training and practice.)

Ninth and tenth graders in the CORS study were asked to design amusement park rides. Students were to consider the appeal of the ride's theme, its size and building materials, the number of people it could carry, its costs, and other related concerns. One girl decided on a water ride with a boat made of balsa wood (rather than pinewood or aluminum). She computed the mass and cost per kilogram of wood as the basis for her decision. Her report specified the size, shape, and construction details of the boat. She used the formula for density to verify that the boat was seaworthy and would carry a 180-pound passenger. Her work showed high analytic skills by focusing on the problem, using higher-order thinking, evaluating alternatives, and clearly interpreting the results to formulate a design.

Two criteria help determine the quality of *disciplined inquiry* in student performance. High quality academic work demonstrates a knowledge and use of *the concepts of a discipline* and employs *elaborated written communication*. Highly proficient work reflects a strong knowledge of subject matter and is communicated in a clear and concise fashion. In a twelfth grade social studies class, for example, CORS study students prepared a paper on U.S. intervention in the Persian Gulf. The following excerpts from one paper demonstrate both the use of disciplinary concepts (cowardly national aggression in recent history) and highly effective written communication. In fact, the sample is also strong in analysis and provides a fitting summary of high quality performance.

> There have been numerous instances when the world has witnessed what happens when aggressors are not stopped. Let us look back to 1935 when Mussolini decided to invade and annex Ethiopia. Ethiopia's emperor appealed to the League of Nations, but nothing was done.
>
> Soon afterwards, in 1936, Adolf Hitler reoccupied the Rhineland, thereby violating the Treaty of Versailles. Again, the world ignored these blatant displays of hostility and power. . . .
>
> When Emperor Hirohito of Japan attacked Manchuria in 1931, and then China in 1937, he was simply scolded by the League of Nations. . . .
>
> In 1938, Hitler united Austria and Germany. The world protested, but then gave in to Hitler who said he only wanted to unite the German people. Then, Hitler took

the Sudentenland from Czechoslovakia. As before, concessions were made to appease the aggressor. . . .

In all the examples of unchecked aggression, the moral is the same. The school bully who demands lunch money from other children will not stop until someone stands up to him. If the bully is allowed to harass, intimidate, and steal from other children, it is giving him silent permission to use power against the weak. . . .

Those who complain about the United States acting as a "police nation" would do well to remember that Desert Storm has been a United Nations effort, not solely a U.S. effort. The U.N. Security Counsel condemned Iraq's invasion and annexation of Kuwait, as did the Arab league. The U.N. imposed mandatory sanctions, forbidding all member states from doing business with Iraq. The European Community, the United States and Japan froze Kuwaiti assets. The United States, Britain, France, Canada, Australia, West Germany, the Netherlands, and Belgium positioned naval vessels to enforce a blockade. . . . Clearly, the United States acted in accordance with the United Nations and with the support of its many members.

There is a time for peace and a time for war. War is a horrible situation, but it is imperative that countries learn to recognize when it is necessary. Perhaps someday the world will be able to solve its problems without violence. In the meantime, we would endanger international security to allow people like Saddam Hussein and his terrorist goons to threaten and overpower independent countries such as Kuwait.

(Source: Wisconsin Center for Educational Research, Madison, WI, 1995.)

Comparative samples of student performance may make the meaning of authentic pedagogy more clear. The following examples are taken from CORS classes of fifth (A) and fifth-sixth graders (B). These work samples were produced by students with identical scores on a test of previous academic success (from the National Assessment of Educational Progress). Example A is a short-answer response exercise from a worksheet about famous explorers. The class devoted 30 minutes to the task and, according to the teacher, the test was typical of what was emphasized in the class. Although the student was graded highly by the teacher, the actual task shows little or no authentic achievement and scores at the very bottom of the CORS authentic assessment and authentic achievement scales.

EXAMPLE A. LOW AUTHENTIC PEDAGOGY
(Source: Wisconsin Center for Educational Research, Madison, WI, 1995.)

99/
A
Super!

① Prince Henry encouraged navigation.

② An important instrument for sea captains was a compass.

③ After Columbus there were many Europeans expeditions to exlpore the Americas.

④ The Aztec and Inca civilizations were destroyed by conquistadors /1

⑤ A legend helped Cortes conquer the Aztecs,

⑥ After Columbus, Europeans started coming to the Americas to live in colonies.

⑦ Europeans who came to the new world included missionaries.

⑧ Several explorers searched for a northwest passage.

Example B is an excerpt from a paper on ecology in fulfillment of an assignment occupying some 40 hours of class time over 12 weeks. Students developed several drafts, each followed by individual consultations with the teacher. The teacher provided students with detailed directions on how to research, organize and write the paper, a step-by-step checklist on the assignment, a sample outline and a sample bibliography format. The paper constituted 75% of each student's quarter grade. The sample paper was seven pages including an overview, information on sea turtle biology, and the hazards they face. Both the task and student achievement rated highly on the CORS scale.

EXAMPLE B. HIGH AUTHENTIC PEDAGOGY
(Source: Wisconsin Center for Educational Research, Madison, WI, 1995.)

The sea turtles are killed for meat and leather, their eggs are taken for food. Their nesting sites are destroyed by man, so they can develop buildings and other places to visit. On some of the beaches they offer boat rides. The boats are located on the sand when they are not being used. The owners are not aware that the boats are resting on top of the sea turtle eggs and killing them.

The sea turtles are classified under two families. The Leatherback and the Regular Sea turtles. The Leatherback Sea Turtles are the largest of the two.

There are alot of unanswered questions today relating to the sea turtles. Despite the explosion of sea turtle research, scientist are frustrated. One of the scientist was quoted saying "I don't know any branch of science where we have applied so much effort and learned so little". "We don't know where each species grows to maturity, or how long it takes them to grow up, or what the survival rates are".

Some of the answers can now be researched because the U.S. and 115 other countries have banned import or export of sea turtle products. By spreading the word and joining support groups, we can also slow down the process.

We can all help by keeping the beaches free of trash and pollution. We can make suggestions to the beach control unit to keep pleasure boating down and only allow it in certain areas where hatching does not take place. Sea turtles have a one percent chance of living to maturity, unlike you and I. We have a greater chance of living a very long life.

AUTHENTIC COGNITIVE APPRENTICESHIPS

Collins, Brown, and Newmann (1989) propose that schools organize cognitive apprenticeships to enable students to participate in the kind of disciplined and productive work that craft opportunities used to provide. We began this chapter by suggesting that the apprenticeship model adapts well to a constructivist view of learning as the personal development of meaning. A fitting medium for such a cognitive apprenticeship is an authentic pedagogy built on the construction of knowledge, disciplined inquiry, and value beyond school. Teachers would serve as mentors and coaches under this conceptualization, actively using students' prior knowledge to promote higher order thinking and in-depth understanding. Teachers would encourage students to express themselves—in conversation and composition, in performance and product.

Resnick and Klopfer (1989) write that cognitive apprenticeships demand three changes in contemporary school practice:

♦ *Cognitive apprenticeships require real tasks* (the construction of knowledge). Students must use prior and new knowledge to confront real problems and issues—a mathematics problem with real hypotheses, or a demanding reading assignment with a related essay. Teachers' talk and evaluation are not enough; they are only adjuncts to real work.

♦ *Cognitive apprenticeships involve contextualized practice.* Students must practice and master entire skills, not just component parts. They might begin with simpler versions of a skill like short essays or less demanding math problems, but eventually they must confront expert performance and learn how to achieve it. Repetitive drill and practice of components, like English usage or math drills, would be little used in apprenticeships.

♦ *Cognitive apprenticeships feature expert performance.* Students need to see others do the kind of academic work they are expected to perform.

> Teachers must make their own mental activities
> transparent. Problem solving practices and writing
> activities must be clear and visible to all. The
> processes of thinking must become overt.

Authentic pedagogy supports a vision and a process that make cognitive apprenticeships feasible. The vision must begin with other elements of personalized education. When teachers know students' developmental levels, their learning/cognitive styles, and their levels of prior knowledge, they are in a position to provide mentoring relationships and helpful advice about suitable learning environments. They can organize for instruction, assessment, and student achievement in ways that promote authenticity in learning.

Personalized education and authentic pedagogy depart significantly from traditional instructional practice geared to conventional tests. Comprehensive studies have yet to be conducted on the impact of authentic pedagogy on traditional test performance; but some recent studies (in six districts) at the elementary school level do support authentic practices. When teachers in these studies taught for understanding and meaning, and connected learning to students' experiences, their students did better than students in traditional classrooms on advanced skills, and as well or better on traditional tests (Knapp, Shields, & Turnbull, 1992).

Some might be concerned that cognitive apprenticeships, personalized education, and authentic learning might diminish traditional curriculum content. In fact, these instructional practices are not concerned with specific content and leave that choice to local agencies. It is possible that greater depth of coverage (rather than extent) might neglect some traditional content, but choices in content are always being made. The superior performance possible under these cognitive-based approaches should outweigh any possible disadvantages. (This is precisely what Sizer (1992) means by his principle, "less is more.")

A great advantage to an authentic approach is that students from all socioeconomic backgrounds tend to be more engaged in authentic work, less in conventional school work. Although teachers can organize instruction in many ways to achieve authentic outcomes, it is our experience and conviction that a highly personalized approach offers the greatest chance for reaching all kinds of students.

ACTION STEPS

- ◆ Generally, school administrators are not experts in pedagogy—of any kind. Contemporary instructional leadership requires this kind of expertise. Read *A Guide to Authentic Instruction and Assessment: Vision, Standards and Scoring* (Newmann, Secada, & Wehlage, Wisconsin Center for Education Research, 1025 West Johnson Street, Madison, WI 53706). Become an expert in authentic pedagogy.

- ◆ Plan a staff development program with your teachers in the concepts and strategies of authentic instruction and assessment.

- ◆ Form a school task force of influential administrators and teacher leaders to plan for the implementation of authentic instructional strategies. Set a timeline and develop a budget. Encourage one or more subject area faculties or interdisciplinary teams to pilot the approach.

5

THE LEARNING ENVIRONMENT

What kinds of learning environments should contemporary schools try to achieve? The question is reminiscent of a story about Abraham Lincoln who responded to comments about the length of his legs by quipping that they were just long enough to reach the ground. Presumably, school learning environments should be good enough to meet the needs of students and reflect contemporary knowledge about learning and instruction. They should be good enough to do the job. But what is the job?

All schools employ horizontal and vertical structures to organize for instruction and learning. Horizontal patterns divide the responsibility for the students among teachers based on several considerations:

- ◆ Curriculum—separate subjects, integrated fields, project approaches, apprenticeships, etc.
- ◆ Teaching arrangements—single subject, teaming, magnet schools or centers, etc.
- ◆ Student groups—large groups, small groups, independent study; heterogeneous groups; homogeneous groups; schools-within-a-school, etc.

Vertical patterns convey students upward from the time of admission to the point of graduation. The most common vertical patterns are these:

- Graded—the traditional age-related plan (pre-school, kindergarten, primary, elementary, middle or junior, secondary).

- Multigraded classroom—students in different grades by subjects (seventh grade in math, eighth grade in language arts, ninth grade in social studies, etc.).

- Nongraded—traditional age/grade levels eliminated and students grouped by achievement levels.

- Cluster—similar to the nongraded plan, but based on content studied or project undertaken rather than achievement.

- Student-driven (continuous progress)—students complete the curriculum at their own pace, level of interest, and level of ability.

The practical nature of instruction has often eluded both scholars and practitioners. The value of any educational structure depends entirely on its utility and efficiency in achieving the goals of instruction. *A particular structure or tactic or strategy is only as good as the results it achieves.* Neither lectures nor group projects nor apprenticeships are good or bad in themselves. The results will reflect the organization of the learning experiences, the level of student motivation, the selection of resources and activities, and an appropriate level of student involvement.

Culture is also a factor. No form of teaching is universally successful. Culture affects how students learn and what they learn. Some scholars believe that children from different cultures perceive and process information differently. All students grow up in cultural contexts that shape their responses. Some cultures reward competitive responses; others, collaborative ones. Cross-gender groups work well in some settings and poorly in others where gender roles are more fixed. Typical classrooms today bring together students from many backgrounds. A teacher cannot hope to be successful with a monolithic or highly bureaucratic approach. The challenge of the contemporary learning environment is diversity. The keys to success are knowledge, flexibility and personalization.

In its 1993 edition of *The Condition of Education*, the U.S. Department of Education's National Center for Education Statistics reported that children of low-income families tend to get stuck in a cycle of low achievement. They progress more slowly and do not get as far as children of high-income families. They are also more likely to drop out of school (NCES, 1993). A vision for change that will work in culturally diverse schools, in schools in low-income areas, and in urban centers, was recently developed by the Regional Educational Laboratory Network (1995). The vision calls for systemic change in six areas:

♦ *School-linked community services*—Schools must foster collaborative social programs serving multiple needs and entire families.

♦ *Culturally compatible schools and classrooms*—Schools must respect and build on the differing value orientations of their students.

♦ *Teachers with high expectations, who care, who are culturally sensitive*—Teachers must be trained to accept and respect children for what they are and to help them grow from their strengths and their prior knowledge and skills.

♦ *Opportunities to learn*—Schools must provide equitable access to content, quality instruction and resources; families must provide support to students and schools.

♦ *School environments that foster resilience*—Resilience is the positive side of "at risk." Schools must protect and support students so that resilience wins out.

♦ *Teacher engagement*—Schools must change the conditions under which teachers work to foster communities of learning (see Chapter 1). Principal leadership is essential for this to happen.

Traditional research on classroom instruction concentrated on the relationship between teacher behaviors and student achievement. Recent research has also emphasized mediating factors—school and classroom climate, student attitudes, motivation, and thought processes. These latter processes mediate between school inputs and outcomes, between instruction and learning. Several of the elements of the Regional Educational Laboratory Network vision are mediating factors—cultural compatibility, teacher expectations, resilient environments, and teacher engagement. We focus here on the impact of learning environments on effective teaching and learning.

LEARNING ENVIRONMENTS

The classroom learning environment has been studied extensively using variations of Moos' (1974) school climate dimensions: relationship, personal development, and system maintenance and change. Knight and Waxman (1991) reported that selected classroom dimensions are related to student academic achievement and to school productivity. Other studies (Waxman & Ellet, 1992) have found that the learning environment in predominantly minority classrooms is significantly different from that in majority classrooms. Black and Hispanic students generally see their learning environments as less favorable than white students in the same classrooms. Case studies by Fraser and Tobin (1992) in Perth, Australia, produced a broad series of assertions about students and teachers that provide good background for our discussion of alternative learning environments. These are the pertinent findings:

♦ *In whole-class settings, a small group of "target" students dominated verbal interactions.* Most whole-class interactions involved only 3–7 students. Typically, the teachers called first on one high achieving student, followed by other aggressive students (with high-risk orientation). The remainder of the students participated very little. The majority of target students in grades 8–10 were boys.

♦ *Teachers tended to direct higher-level cognitive questions to target students.* Lower-level questions were asked almost at random. More able students were given much more opportunity to develop interactive skills and received positive feedback for their responses.

♦ *Target students held more favorable perceptions of the learning environment than nonparticipant students.* Target students experienced greater involvement in whole-class, small group, and individualized activities, and more freedom in the application of rules than nonparticipants. In fact, target and nonparticipant students seemed to operate in different learning environments within the same classroom.

♦ *Exemplary teachers used management activities which facilitated sustained student engagement.* These teachers had orderly classes characterized by a relaxed atmosphere and good interactions.

♦ *Exemplary teachers used strategies designed to increase student understanding.* Teachers stressed strong student involvement in academic tasks and high verbal interaction.

♦ *Exemplary teachers utilized strategies which encouraged students to participate actively in learning activities.* Teachers found ways to "make it safe" for all students to participate in whole-class, small-group, and individualized activities. Students were treated with respect and given time and support to participate.

♦ *Exemplary teachers maintained favorable classroom learning environments.* These environments were high in involvement, teacher support, and order and organization.

These findings suggest that traditional classroom environments are less than ideal for all but a few high achieving or more aggressive students. They also show that exemplary teachers encourage student engagement, participation, and understanding.

If conventional classroom environments and traditional teaching are not very supportive of student academic growth, what kinds of teaching and learning environments are needed?

A HISTORICAL EXAMPLE—THE JOHN DEWEY SCHOOL

The concept of child-centered education originated with Jean-Jacques Rousseau in 18th century France and was translated to American schools via the ideas of Johann Pestalozzi and Friedrick Froebel (disciples of Rousseau) and the efforts of Francis Parker and John Dewey. Parker was the founder of what came to be called "progressive education," which Dewey popularized.

John Dewey was a philosopher, psychologist, and educator at the University of Chicago and later at Columbia University. While at Chicago, he formed a Laboratory School (in 1896) that was guided by three general principles:

♦ Instruction must concentrate on developing students' minds, not on subject matter;

♦ Instruction must be project-oriented and integrated, not segmented into small units of time (40 or 50 minutes per subject).

♦ Curriculum must progress through the years of schooling from practical experiences (gardening or cooking) to formal subjects (botany or home-making) to integrated studies (agriculture or home economics in the American culture).

The Dewey School was developed around *occupations* to encourage students to start with what was interesting and useful to them. Progress then was to more formal academic topics that still had a relationship to the real world. Notice that this vision of schooling was *authentic*—committed to active learning, construction of knowledge, use of prior knowledge, problem-solving, and values beyond school. Projects were organized to realize four criteria: (1) hands-on activities; (2) scientific processes (observing, analyzing, investigating, quantifying, and making predictions); (3) social cooperation; and (4) exchange of ideas. Projects included such activities as building a clubhouse, planting a crop, researching and understanding the reasons for the founding and development of the city of Chicago, and the study of light and optics through photography.

Dewey believed that reading and writing should be stressed from the initial days of school with formal instruction in the symbol system postponed until young children understood why it was needed. Drill and practice were embedded in real tasks for both language and mathematics. For learning new vocabulary, teachers wrote sentences on the blackboard for children to read after they talked about real-world activities. Students discovered number principles by counting objects, using a ruler, etc. (For more details on the Dewey School, see Sylvia Farnham-Diggory, 1992).

The Dewey School was both visionary and successful, but its principles were hard to implement. Training teachers in sufficient numbers to implement Dewey's ideas and methods was daunting. Training for the behavioral classroom proved easier and eclipsed Dewey's model in time. The principles remain valid, however, and can be incorporated in a cognitive apprenticeship.

A CONTEMPORARY MODEL—THE COGNITIVE APPRENTICESHIP

Allan Collins and John Seely Brown have formulated a new kind of educational system which they call *cognitive apprenticeship* (Brown, Collins, & Duguid, 1989; Collins, Brown, & Newmann, 1989). The model is not yet fully developed, but its general outline suggests that it will be one of the dominant models of schooling in the 21st century.

Table 5.1 illustrates the framework of the cognitive apprenticeship as proposed by Collins and Brown. The framework has four categories and multiple subsets. We briefly discuss each of these categories.

1. *Content*—Subject matter knowledge and three kinds of procedural knowledge.

    - *Domain Knowledge*—Forms of declarative, conceptual and analogical knowledge usually associated with textbooks, lectures, and projects. Collins and Brown called this

TABLE 5.1. THE COGNITIVE APPRENTICESHIP FRAMEWORK
(Source: Collins, Brown, & Newman, 1989, as cited in *Cognitive Processes in Education*, Second Edition, by Sylvia Farnham-Diggory, 1992, p. 568. Reprinted by permission of Harper Collins College Publisher.)

Content
Domain Knowledge
Problem-Solving Strategies
Control Strategies
Learning Strategies

Methods
Modeling
Scaffolding and Fading
Articulation
Reflection
Exploration

Sequence
Global Before Local Skills
Increasing Complexity
Increasing Diversity

Sociology
Situated Learning
Culture of Expert Practice
Intrinsic Motivation
Cooperation versus Competition

knowledge "inert" because it does not *produce* anything. Traditional schools specialize in inert knowledge. It is necessary, but preliminary.

- *Procedural Knowledge*—(1) *Problem-solving strategies and heuristics* which are methods of teaching that encourage students to experiment and to discover information for themselves, such as learning to *speak* a foreign language; (2) *Control strategies* which involve *metacognition*—the monitoring, diagnosing and self-checking that are used by expert learners; and (3) *Learning strategies*, the tasks involved in acquiring knowledge and skills in a domain.

2. *Methods*—No one can learn for anyone; they must do it for themselves. Teachers must constantly resist the urge to spoon-feed students. Teachers learn from lectures, because they must organize the information. Students are not so fortunate, because their role is typically passive. To offset this, Collins and Brown suggest six active teaching methods that fall into three groups:

    • *Processes of Observation and Guided Practice*—(1) *Modeling* which involves showing a student how to do something. In abstract processes, this means *talking about* the reasoning or problem-solving processes so that students can see how they operate; (2) *Coaching* in which the student performs a task and the teacher provides feedback. Coaching is prompting some aspect of working memory, about goals, cues, retrieval of knowledge, etc; (3) *Scaffolding and Fading* which is furnishing a cognitive support for something a student cannot yet do (e.g., providing a detailed outline for writing a composition) and then removing it when the student shows sufficient independence. Cooperative problem solving encompasses all three of these methods; i.e., a teacher models an activity and coaches her students while providing scaffolds to get them started.

- *Processes of Focused Attention and Cognitive Control*—(1) *Articulation* which requires students to verbalize or demonstrate learning through discussion or critiques. This is an extension of the old saying that teaching something is the best way to learn it. Talking about one's knowledge both clarifies and reinforces learning; (2) *Reflection* involves a replay of performance. Either the teacher personally shows a student what he or she is doing or uses a videotape or computer simulation. Athletic coaching is heavily dependent on this method.

- *Processes of Exploration* in which students try out other domains to apply their newly acquired knowledge and skills. Arts programs often utilize this method.

3. *Sequence*—Students are shown the proper ordering of tasks. Collins and Brown propose three principles of sequencing:

  - *Global Before Local*—Novices must see the big picture before going on to subskills or sub-components of a task. Musicians, artists and athletics often gain experience from someone else's (expert) performance before attempting a new activity or skill. Again, recordings and computer simulations can be very helpful.

  - *Increasing Complexity*—Initial skills should anticipate and prepare the student for more complex skills so that, as performance becomes more automatic, learners can attend to other, more complex objectives. This is exactly the way most novices learn to drive or paint a picture or give a speech.

- *Increasing Diversity*—This is the issue of *transfer*, how to apply one's learning and skills in different contexts and settings. Transfer of learning is not automatic. Novices must learn, for example, how to apply the abstract rules of problem solving in increasingly diverse and complicated settings.

4. *Sociology*—The character of the learning environment for the cognitive apprentice. Collins and Brown discuss four factors that introduce the novice to the culture and community of expert practice.

   - *Situated Learning*—Learning made meaningful by actual experience. Situated learning encompasses both the physical and sociocultural elements of the learning environment. Brown, et al. (1989), emphasize that students must learn the knowledge and skills—the tools—of a discipline as real practitioners, not as elementary or secondary school students. This implies working in real or simulated environments of the actual discipline.

   - *Culture of Expert Practice*—Students must be exposed to working practitioners of a discipline using the tools of the discipline in the actual working environment. Some magnet schools have been successful in creating such environments and Tech-Prep programs attempt to provide transition from the simulated environment of the school to the actual world of professional preparation and practice.

   - *Intrinsic Motivation*—Students engaged in learning life-related knowledge and skills will not be satisfied with external forms of motivation (praise, grades, rewards), but must come to an (internal) sense of satisfaction like that experienced by working adults.

- *Cooperation versus Competition*—Most modern achievements have been won by groups of people collaborating on mutual goals. Competition can provide incentive and even a basis for differentiating work roles, but real-world performance involves persons with different jobs and skills and functions working together to do a job.

An apprenticeship requires a suitable learning environment to achieve the content, methods, sequence, and sociology of an adult or adult-like workplace. Sylvia Farnham-Diggory (1992) cites as an example of an exemplary cognitive apprenticeship a "topic study" curriculum published by the Jordanhill College of Education in Glasgow, Scotland. "Topic study" was created by Fred Rendell to integrate the disciplines of reading, writing, spelling, literature, social studies, mathematics, science, and art. The curriculum, called *Whale*, is currently in use in the upper elementary and lower secondary grades of Scotland's schools. *Whale* has 10 units intended to be taught for several hours each day over about 3 months' time. Each unit begins with a story and uses experiments, research, art, media, writing, and multiple representations to explore the relationships between men and whales through the ages. A teacher's manual, a resource book, and five user-friendly computer discs provide text, activities, maps, sketches, archival data, and 25 computer programs to create the apprenticeship environment. Teachers use modeling, coaching, and scaffolding methods to support student articulation, reflection, and exploration. Students work in small groups on increasingly complex and diverse projects, using research, models, and computers to solve real problems—all without formal grades.

TACTICS AND PATTERNS

An enormous amount of research and field study has been undertaken to assess the knowledge base of teaching and instruction. Walberg (1984, 1990) has admirably summarized this vast literature under the mantle of school productivity. Much of this work reflects the behavioral model and we refer interested readers to Walberg's syntheses for detailed information. Walberg's quantitative analyses and case studies define nine factors in three groups that are the most powerful influences on cognitive, affective and behavioral learning. *Aptitude* factors include (1) ability or prior achievement on standardized tests, (2) development or age, and (3) motivation or self-concept. *Instructional* factors include (4) the amount of time engaged in learning, and (5) the quality of the instructional experience. *Environmental* factors include (6) the home, (7) the classroom, (8) the peer group outside school, and (9) out-of-school use of time (in particular, television viewing).

The strongest *instructional* effects in the Walberg research resulted from Skinnerian reinforcement techniques, acceleration programs, reading training, instructional cues, engagement and corrective feedback, mastery learning (in science), and cooperative learning. Graded homework and class morale rated highest among the *environmental* influences. These and other elements and methods of teaching can be combined in patterns.

Behavioral laboratory and classroom research from the 1950s through the 1970s produced the model or pattern known as "Explicit Teaching" which is intended to make traditional whole-class teaching more productive. Behavioral researchers do not all agree on the appropriate name or components of this pattern, calling it variously process-product, direct, active, and effective teaching. In any event, Rosenshine and Stevens (1986) identified six fundamental "functions" of this model:

♦ Daily review, checking of previous day's work and homework, and reteaching, if necessary;

♦ Presentation of new content and skills in small steps;

- Guided student practice and checking for understanding, with close teacher monitoring;
- Feedback and correctives, and reteaching if necessary;
- Independent student practice in seatwork and homework (the goal is a 90% success rate); and
- Weekly and monthly reviews with frequent tests, and reteaching, if necessary.

Cognitive research of the 1980s to the present revived and expanded earlier work on student-centered and higher-order learning to produce another, more independent approach to instruction. This so-called "Comprehension Teaching" flows from the work of Russian psychologist Lev Vygotsky (1962) who identified a "zone of proximal development" in learning that extends from what learners can do independently to what they can do with teacher help. This cognitive approach utilizes "scaffolding" techniques to help students build knowledge, and "fading" (removing the scaffolding) to encourage student self-monitoring and independence.

David Pearson outlines three phases of teaching for comprehension:

- *Modeling*—The teacher demonstrates the desired behavior;
- *Guided Practice*—Students work with teacher help; and
- *Application*—Students act independently of the teacher.

Some teacher functions of Explicit Teaching—planning, allocation of time, and reviewing—are also used in Comprehension Teaching to foster student self-direction and independence. Comprehension Teaching has its own distinctive functions, however, ones that reflect its cognitive nature. We consider three tactics of this pattern in more detail.

SCAFFOLDING

A scaffold is a temporary cognitive support provided by a teacher or another student to bridge the gap between a student's present knowledge or skills and the defined goal of the learning. A scaffold can be used for modeling, guided practice, or application. It is gradually removed as the student becomes more independent. Scaffolding is only applicable within a student's "zone of proximal development"—that area where the student cannot act independently, but can perform with teacher help. The first task of the teacher is to establish the bounds of this zone and whether all students have the prior knowledge to do the work as defined.

Various kinds of scaffolds have appeared in the literature (Palincsar & Brown, 1984; Rosenshine & Guenther, 1992). Rosenshine and Guenther list nine scaffolds or cognitive facilitators that research shows support student learning:

Presentational

- Developing specific scaffolds to help students learn a skill;
- Regulating the difficulty by starting with simpler materials and gradually increasing the complexity;
- Modeling the steps and the thought processes of a skill;
- Thinking out loud (another form of modeling);
- Anticipating and discussing potential student errors;

Guided Practice

- Using reciprocal teaching (more on this later);
- Providing cue cards containing the steps of a scaffold (see Table 5.2);

- Furnishing half-finished examples to reduce initial complexity (How are ____ and ____ alike?)

Feedback

- Providing checklists to be used in evaluating work.

TABLE 5.2. SCAFFOLD TO SUMMARIZE A PARAGRAPH
(Source: Rosenshine & Guenther, 1992)

---

1. Identify the topic.
2. Write two or three words that reflect the topic.
3. Use these words as a prompt to figure out the main idea of the paragraph (see Baumann, 1984).
4. Select two details that elaborate on the main idea and are important to remember.
5. Write two or three sentences that best incorporate these important ideas (see Taylor & Frye, 1988).

The strategy outlined in Table 5.2 is a typical scaffold. It could be used as an introductory presentation to help students learn how to summarize. It could also be produced as a cue-card or as a feedback checklist. In any event, it would be available to students at whatever stage of the process they needed help—bridging from what they already know to the level of a new skill.

RECIPROCAL TEACHING

Palincsar and Brown (1984) developed a set of cognitive strategies derived from Vygotskian theory to help students understand written text. Reciprocal teaching involves a teacher in explicitly modeling the routines of dialogue and discussion—questioning, clarifying, summarizing, and predicting.

First, students read a text and then the teacher and a group of students take turns leading the discussion on what has been read. The leader (teacher or student) begins the discussion by asking questions and encouraging student involvement. The leader's job is to explain, clarify, and ultimately summarize the discussion. If the group cannot agree on the meaning, they reread the text and engage in additional questioning and discussion until consensus is reached.

The process is entirely cooperative and collegial. Each student takes a turn in leading the group and in guiding the dialogue. Initially, the teacher models and guides the process (scaffolding). This teacher modeling provides examples of expert performance. As students become more familiar with the tactics, they initiate more and more of the discussion themselves. The *reciprocal* nature of the process encourages student engagement. Students assume the roles of planning and monitoring traditionally exercised by teachers.

The research of Palincsar and Brown has demonstrated significant achievement gains in reading comprehension by at-risk students when reciprocal teaching is employed. Approximately 80% of 287 junior high school students and 366 primary grade students raised their text comprehension scores from about 30% correct to the 75–80% range on five successive tests (Brown & Campione, 1992). Students maintained this level of competence even a year after the reciprocal teaching was completed. Most of this work was originally conducted with disadvantaged middle school students, but it has been extended to high school and junior college settings. Brown and Campione also found considerable transfer value in the processes that students mastered, particularly in three areas: (1) generalization to content-area settings; (2) improved performance on posttests geared to the strategies; and (3) significantly improved performance on standardized tests (2 years on average).

In typical reading groups, students simply practice to read. They read one unrelated text after another with little or no opportunity to establish coherence or cumulative meaning. In reciprocal teaching classrooms, students read to build a coherent body of knowledge. They read to understand and write and teach. They read to learn; not just learn to read.

Brown and Campione (1992) cite a reciprocal teaching/learning discussion among four sixth graders in a science class about the *Exxon Valdez* oil spill. The discussion on the topic, "Kelp Keeps Everybody Happy," went like this:

Student 1: Why do scientists think most of the sea otters will die?

Student 2: Because they live mostly in that section. So when the oil gets on their fur, they'll sink or get too cold. And it gets in their stomachs where they try to lick themselves clean—or drown or something.

Student 3: (*Clarification*) We're missing the boring old chain stuff.

Student 1: We're getting there.

Student 4: (*Explanation*) Oil kills otters, otters eat sea urchins, sea urchins eat kelp. Kelp keeps everyone happy. Take out otters, and you've got one of those broken links. Too many of some—not enough of another.

Student 2: (*Clarification*) Another problem, it says here, is the oil on top of the water makes it dark. It's dark, and the sun can't get in, so it doesn't grow.—What doesn't grow?

Student 3: (*Summary*) The plankton is hurt because it has no sun for energy, so the shrimp's not fed and the tuna's not fed, because it eats the shrimp, and so on in a circle—or a web?

Student 1: (*Prediction*) I predict that all of the otters and other sea life will be endangered if this goes on.

(Source: "Students as Researchers and Teachers" by Ann L. Brown and Joseph C. Compione, in *Teaching for Thinking*, edited by J. W. Keefe and H.J. Walberg, 1992. Reprinted with permission of the National Association of Secondary School Principals, Reston, VA.)

In this science classroom, students pursued an environmental science curriculum that emphasized depth of coverage over breadth, using scientific inquiry and the general skills of literacy. Students did library research, conducted experiments, participated in field trips, and collected and analyzed various data around central themes like balance, adaptation, competition, and cooperation. Learning was supported by collaborative student activities, cooperative groups based on the Jigsaw methodology, and state-of-the-art technology. Reciprocal teaching works well in reading but, as this science example shows, it also works in content areas that demand reading, writing, and problem-solving and thinking skills.

COACHING

Farnham-Diggory (1994) argues that there are only four basic teaching methods: (1) *talking* (lecturing, questioning); (2) *displaying* (modeling, demonstrating); (3) *coaching* (cuing, guiding); and (4) *arranging the learning environment*. Almost all teaching depends on all four methods, regardless of the various tactics that are used. Traditional teaching relies heavily on the first and second methods, while cognitive approaches use all four, particularly the third and fourth. Indeed, coaching and arranging the learning environment are often interrelated. Coaching is more successful if the learning environment is friendly, supportive, resource-rich, and interactive.

Cognitive proponents favor learning by doing, using knowledge to solve problems, and skill in application of reading, writing, and thinking for meaning. But students need help—what some call "guided practice" or, better yet, "coached practice" (Lesgold, 1988). Coaching has a long history in modern school reform. The concept appeared as "facilitation" in the NASSP Model Schools Project (1969–1974) and is a major feature of the Theodore Sizer Coalition of Essential Schools and Re: Learning initiatives, and the just released NASSP/Carnegie Foundation report, *Breaking Ranks: Changing an American Institution* (1996).

Coaching is prompting and questioning, as well as guiding and supervising practice. Coaching must be directed to aspects of students' working memories—goal setting, awareness of cues, retrieval of knowledge, the actual performance, and self-monitoring. In coaching, the teacher guides a student in the performance of a task with the goal of achieving competence closer to expert performance. Remember how athletic and dance and singing coaches work with their students. The student tries a skill or activity and the coach critiques and makes suggestions for improvement (feedback). To learn, a student must construct a *working memory program* for that task. Coaching is directed to improving these working memory programs. The teacher must suggest a different goal, point out missed cues, model different ways of performing, or provide ways for students to self-monitor their performance.

Teachers using Topic Studies in the schools of Scotland, for example, spend a great amount of time analyzing the difficulties that students are experiencing. They model ways that students can analyze their own learning difficulties (coach themselves). Similarly, Schoenfeld (1985) believes in using two- or three-person groups in mathematics for students to work cooperatively on problems. He regularly asks these questions of students and even posts them in the classroom:

- What exactly are you doing? Can you describe it precisely?

- Why are you doing it? How does it fit the solution?

- How does it help you? What will you do with the outcome when you obtain it?

Schoenfeld begins instruction by thinking aloud as he solves a new problem (modeling) and then has the students work cooperatively in small groups as he guides and supervises them. At first, students cannot answer his three questions, but learn, almost in self-defense, to confront them because they know that he will ask them again and again. The goal, of course, is habitual behavior and more expert performance.

Contemporary cognitive researchers conceptualize coaching in terms of problem-solving and propose various new roles for teachers. Bransford and Vye (1989) summarize these problem-solving roles in six categories:

♦ Coaches monitor and supervise students' attempts at problem-solving, not only to prevent students from going too far into a flawed solution, but also to give them adequate experience in the complexities and turns of real problem-solving. Schoenfeld's approach allows students to really experience mathematical problem solving without early intervention; computer intelligent tutoring systems tend to intervene earlier to keep students from too much frustration.

♦ Coaches help students reflect on their problem solving processes and contrast them with the approaches of others. This may entail having students think out loud during problem-solving, or discuss attempts after the fact, or model the strategies for students. Bransford, et al. (1988), calls this providing a model of "intelligent novices"—the teacher displaying his or her own *imperfect* attempts at problem solving.

♦ Coaches use problem-solving tasks for assessment. This is classic diagnosis in personalized education. Teachers identify what students can already do by letting them solve problems and then provide feedback. Good computer-based instruction, for example, diagnoses errors and misconceptions as the foundation for successful performance.

♦ Coaches use problem-solving exercises to create "teachable moments" by giving students opportunities to compare and contrast their own ideas with other possibilities. Posner, et al. (1982), argue that cognitive change requires (1) that students be dissatisfied with their existing ideas; (2) that they have at least minimal understanding of an alternative way of thinking; (3) that the alternative way must be plausible; and (4) that students must see the alternative as applicable to various situations. The key element here is for students to experience new ways of thinking as guides to their own thinking.

♦   Coaches choose coherent problem-solving experiences that help students achieve overall meaningful comprehension. Palincsar and Brown, for example, used meaningful and related texts in their studies to further students' knowledge as they learned to read; not unrelated exercises that provided no context or continuity.

♦   Coaches may be either classroom teachers or computer-based intelligent tutoring systems or other students. Cooperation of various kinds is important to prepare students for the give and take of real life.

We could offer many other examples of Teaching for Comprehension that incorporate constructivist and personalized perspectives. *Cooperative learning* for example, is a widely used method that affords good cognitive and affective performance for the majority of students (Slavin, 1991). *Simulation and role playing* are excellent tactics for actively engaging students in interpretation and the making of meaning. *Project learning,* like Odyssey of the Mind (and science fairs), stimulates student initiative, creativity and problem-solving. *Case study approaches* encourage students to confront information about real-world situations and to solve problems based on their analyses. The challenge here is to inspire teachers to move beyond "covering the curriculum" and traditional instruction to placing the student in charge of the learning process. Cognitive-based approaches to teaching and learning require a paradigm-shift in our views of learning and learners.

MANAGEMENT OF THE LEARNING ENVIRONMENT

The learning environment, whether a classroom, or a resource center, or an apprenticeship experience, is a workplace that requires managing if it is to be safe, supportive, and productive. Management in this case is simply running the learning environment. Teachers must exercise certain executive functions if they and their students are to be successful. These executive functions, according to Berliner (1989), include: planning, communicating goals; regulating the activities of the workplace; creating a pleasant environment for work; educating new members of the work group; relating the work of the site to the other units in the system; supervising and working with other people; motivating those being supervised; and evaluating the performance of those being supervised. We limit our discussion to those elements of management that directly affect learning and instruction.

Planning is fundamental to an organized and productive learning environment. Berliner (1989) suggests that planning includes selecting content within district and school guidelines, scheduling the use of time, forming groups that are defensible and flexible, and choosing tasks and activities for learning and instruction. Clearly, teachers must plan if all students are to be served. The activity structures that teachers plan are particularly important. An approach heavy in lecturing and recitation places the teacher at the center of learning and can readily result in (and reward) passive behavior on the part of the students. More active forms of learning and instruction, such as small groups and project work, place the student more at the center. These approaches are more suited to cognitive patterns like Teaching for Comprehension. The problem with more active learning patterns, however, is that the teacher must be well-organized and highly involved to prevent and respond to student misbehavior or inattention to task.

Goal communication is equally important. Berliner (1989) recommends that teachers pay careful attention to structuring the features and sequence of instruction and to setting and communicating high expectations for student performance. Students tend to be more successful when teachers discuss the goals of a learning activity and let them know clearly what they are expected to do. This is not to suggest that structuring should be overdone. Too many procedures and rules can take valuable time from learning and dismotivate students from accepting responsibility for their own learning. Expectations, however, can rarely be too high. When teachers exhibit high, but attainable expectations, many studies show that students achieve better academic success and better attendance and behavior.

Regulating the activities of the school learning environment involves controlling the pace of instruction, sequencing the various activities, monitoring student success, managing the use of learning time, establishing a safe, orderly and business-like working environment, and preventing or handling student behavior problems. Of these activities, student success rate, time management and an orderly workplace are crucial to productivity. Success rate is particularly important during the early phases of learning, during recitation, and small-group work. Findings from the Beginning Teacher Evaluation Study, for example, support a relationship between a high success rate for younger and less academically advantaged students and improved test performance and satisfaction (see Berliner, 1989, p. 110).

Time use is also directly related to successful learning. Too much time spent in transitions, or distributing materials, or even disciplining students can add up rapidly. Again, the Beginning Teacher Evaluation Study found that "academic learning time," when students work *with success* on defined learning objectives, is the key to productive student achievement.

An orderly workplace is the foundation for a successful learning environment, just as it is for a functioning business or professional office. The effective schools research has shown time and again that student achievement is higher when order and focus are present. Brookover, et al. (1982), offer a list of management techniques that facilitate instruction, increase the effective use of time, and reduce student misbehavior. Many of these techniques—fluency of transitions, use of student monitors, standardized routines, early intervention in misbehavior, group focus, etc.—directly promote order and purpose in the learning environment. Staff development, of course, is critical to learning and using these strategies. And, of course, these strategies must be practiced.

Management techniques are a means to an end and not an end in themselves. It is possible to pervert the academic purpose of the learning environment by too much control. Teachers can be too much concerned with getting the job done and not enough with the quality of the task. Strong control can result in high engagement, but limited learning. Balance is needed so that students perceive the structure and support, yet feel free to strive for self-direction and independence in their learning. Evidence exists that an ordered system is prerequisite to higher cognitive instruction. Soar and Soar (1983) discovered a difference, for example, between teachers' control of student behavior and their control of learning tasks. Research in elementary schools showed that these functions were correlated, but related differentially to student learning. Behavioral control and achievement were related in a linear fashion (more is better) whereas control of learning tasks and achievement showed a curvilinear relationship (an inverted U). Apparently, an *intermediate* amount of teacher control over student learning tasks is most effective, especially for more gifted students on higher cognitive tasks. Teachers need to exercise good control to support student commitment to learning while encouraging flexibility in the process of learning. For example, activities like project and lab work and strategies such as cooperative small group learning allow students considerable flexibility in their learning tasks yet provide sufficient structure to keep learning and performance on task.

Order in the learning environment is defined by the quality of the academic activities that teachers and students collaboratively develop. Doyle (1986, p. 424) tells us that "the key to a teacher's success in management appears to be his or her (a) understanding of the likely configuration of events in a classroom, and (b) skill in monitoring and guiding activities in light of this information. From this perspective, management effectiveness cannot be defined solely in terms of rules for behavior. Effectiveness must also include such cognitive dimensions as comprehension and interpretation, skills which are necessary for recognizing when to act and how to improvise classroom events to meet immediate circumstances."

ACTION STEPS

♦ Observe and analyze teacher-student interactions in three classrooms of your school. Do teachers call primarily on high achieving and aggressive students ("target" students)? Interview the teachers and probe the reasons for their actions.

♦ Visit a school that features a topic study approach or a project approach in at least some of its classrooms. (Ask a few of your colleagues or a professor for some recommendations.) Write up the salient characteristics of these learning environments.

♦ Using the examples cited in this chapter as models, develop a scaffold to teach students the steps of critical problem solving based on a resource such as *Tactics for Thinking* by Marzano and Arredondo, (ASCD, 1986).

♦ With members of your school staff or a group of colleagues, use a reciprocal teaching strategy to explore the meaning of the cognitive apprenticeship. Read the work of Palincsar and Brown or Brown and Campione as background for your discussion.

♦ Interview a teacher who employs coaching as a primary instructional tactic. Observe his or her learning environment. How does it differ from the conventional classroom?

6

SUBJECT MATTER INSTRUCTION AND ASSESSMENT

Our discussion to this point has treated instruction and the learning environment in a general way. In this chapter, we explore current instructional trends in English, the arts, mathematics, science, and the social sciences. Where possible, specific information is offered about staff development opportunities for teachers. We also discuss new trends in instructional assessment.

All instruction should be personalized to fit the learning style and developmental level of individual students, but some current trends appear to run through all major efforts to improve instruction. These trends are general enough to have implications for each subject in the school curriculum.

Teaching for understanding: The practice of memorizing discrete information in preparation for the weekly or unit test appears to be inconsistent with the national reports which call for a more general competency in problem-solving and higher order thinking skills among all students. Learning is more than memorization and often involves the ability to apply knowledge and skills in predictable and unpredictable situations (Gardner, 1993).

Symbol analysts and generators of new knowledge: Secretary of Labor Robert Reich uses both of these terms to describe the newest developmental tasks of youth (to borrow a term from the work of Robert Havighurst). In an information-driven world the future belongs to those persons who can make sense of the myriad of symbol systems which they encounter daily and even more so to the individuals who can decipher the symbols and use them in the generation of new knowledge. New knowledge is created when extant knowledge is combined in interesting ways. This process is enhanced measurably when the structures are broadened by which concepts in any discipline are considered.

Teaching in context: A major responsibility of instruction is to assist students to see the connection between the subject matter which they are asked to learn and the real world. Teaching must emphasize the values embedded in learning content. Instruction appropriately begins by relating the content and skills to be learned with their utility. The closer the relevance to the individual student, the more powerful the motivation for learning the material.

Teaching for thinking: Figuring out what to do when you don't know what to do is one way to describe what will be required of all students to participate in a rapidly changing society and world. It seems no longer tenable to expect higher order thinking only of students whose early environments prepared them for higher level course material. Reflective thinking, once exclusive turf for students in advanced classes, now becomes an imperative for all students.

Collaboration as a means for learning: One well-validated approach to classroom instruction with implications for all subjects is cooperative learning. Now that American businesses have endorsed the value of having workers who can cooperate as well as compete, the idea of cooperation in learning has had a rebirth. Based on the work of David and Roger Johnson at the University of Minnesota and Robert Slavin at the Johns Hopkins University, collaborative group teaching strategies are becoming more visible in classrooms regardless of subject matter. With the proliferation of technology, it is now possible for learning teams to involve students from different schools and even different countries in solutions to common problems.

Technology as a tool for learning: The accelerated growth of technology and technological resources restricts possibilities for learning only to the limits of our imaginations. CD-ROMs enable students to hear the written words of great men and women as they read them. Networking with worldwide databases enables teachers and students to connect with primary source materials. The Internet expands the opportunities for interaction across states and countries so that students can communicate directly with students, teachers, researchers, and experts. Software can present drill and practice activities. Calculators can reduce students' needs to commit algorithms and formulas to memory. The world of technology permits interaction to assume new meanings far exceeding conventional face-to-face communication.

ENGLISH/LANGUAGE ARTS

Years have passed since James Moffet wrote *Student Centered Language Arts.* At the time of its publication it advocated a radical approach to the teaching of English and related areas. Moffet suggested that teachers of English include more hands-on experiences in which students engaged content directly as they worked solo, in pairs, or in inquiry groups. Among his recommendations for enlivening the subject were such provocations as journal writing, reporting, sensory recording, script writing, stream-of-consciousness writing, reflective poetry and thematic teaching. He argued that skills are best learned in context and not *a priori* to their application. Moffet's recommendations were a harbinger of things to come in the teaching of English.

National standards for the language arts call for relating what is learned to one's own life. For example, the following two standards taken from the *Standards Project for English Language Arts* (1992) expect students to be able to apply what they are learning in literature to their writing. The student:

Identifies specific stylistic and rhetorical characteristics of "good" literature and utilizes them in his/her own writing (e.g. descriptive phrases, use of foreshadowing);

Uses specific pieces of literature as vehicles for future writing topic development.

In addition to literature as a source of writing content and style, students are urged to base descriptive writing on the careful observation of real events. Careful, patient observation is not the exclusive currency of the scientist, but the grist for good writing as well. The famous haiku poet Basho wrote, "When we observe calmly, all things have their fulfillment." Sharpening the powers of observation enables students to see more subtle nuances of meaning and increase the likelihood of writing with great breadth and depth.

Literature can also enable students to look more analytically at the human experience and in so doing learn, practice and/or reinforce a very valuable cognitive processing skill. If one were to have students read the very popular modern work, *The Bridges of Madison County*, they could be asked to analyze the personality structures of the protagonists, Francesca and Robert Kincaid. Were they compatible? Was their meeting a chance encounter which grew out of each one's loneliness? How might life have been for each if she had chosen to go with him? Why do you think she chose to remain at home with her family? How might you have reacted if you were her children? Such analyses can be accomplished in cooperative groups, pairs or independently. The main point, however, is that students would put literature to use rather than merely enduring it.

Writing across the curriculum describes the value of having all teachers, regardless of the subjects they teach, emphasize good writing skills. How students explain data in science or develop a game plan for a physical activity exemplifies the power of written language. Persuasive writing in the social studies, business, or even mathematics attempts to convince others to accept a point of view, buy a product, or adopt a strategy for solving a problem. Approached in this manner, all students can see value in the written word and become aware of their powers and talents. They can also see that writing well and purposely is exhilarating.

The project approach to writing enables students to select from a list of options which, when collated, produce a general work that is greater than the sum of its parts. Most readers are familiar with *The Foxfire Book* produced by students in a high school English class. Of similar worth are local histories written by students after considerable investigation into a community's background. Scientific investigations can result in books about a particular environment or habitat. Several high schools are now requiring some type of formal paper or thesis as a performance requirement for graduation. These papers can be completed in groups or individually, but hold each student accountable for using the language arts effectively.

English/language arts students can enhance skills by completing software packages on spelling, mechanics, and grammar. They can use laptop computers and word processing programs complete with spell checkers and grammar checkers for creating their compositions. Teachers can access databases for enriching content and for personalizing instruction. They may also soon find that grading students' compositions and essays can be accomplished effectively using computers (Page & Petersen, 1995).

MATHEMATICS

Understanding mathematics means more than applying correct procedures to generate right answers. The National Research Council called the practice of step-by-step mathematics "mindless mimicry mathematics" (National Research Council, 1989). Ironically, the "new" mathematics seems similar to the mathematics of 1958 when, in the shadow of Sputnik, the Federal government implemented the National Defense Education Act. Inquiry-based education was seen in such instructional and curricular innovations as the School Mathematics Study Group (SMSG) and the University of Illinois Curriculum Study in Mathematics (UICSM). Both of these projects were aimed at helping students learn the structure of the discipline and develop mathematical habits of mind.

In light of new discoveries about how students learn generally and mathematics specifically, the focus has changed from rote, regurgitation and recitation to one of making sense of the mathematical ideas students are asked to learn. Teaching based on constructivism focuses on the meanings that each student brings to the learning environment and his or her readiness for conceptual advancement. Rather than looking for the right answers, teachers of mathematics are implored to examine the wrong answers that students present for the cognitive structure out of which the answer was produced. When students answer a problem incorrectly, it is the function of the teacher to discover the question they indeed answered correctly.

The beginnings of successful teaching in mathematics are students' *present* cognitive structures in the field. Students learn some mathematics in the process of their childhood. They learn more in the process of formal schooling. They also learn to perceive themselves on a continuum of competency as either strong, weak or somewhere in between. Children, regardless of their home curriculum, typically arrive at the kindergarten door excited and anxious about the myriad possibilities of schooling. For too many students, however, school is no longer viewed as a positive place by the time they reach high school. This is especially true for the mathematics classroom, largely because students' intuitive ideas about mathematics are rejected in favor of getting the right answers.

Moving to a problem-solving approach to instruction means eschewing the textbook and standardized testing mentality which has plagued traditional mathematics instruction. Just as there was no royal road to Rome, frequently there are as many ways to arrive at a mathematical answer as there are students in the classroom. Asking students to invent their own solutions to problems and then to defend their procedures before a jury of their peers is the stuff of which real learning is made. Informed mathematics teachers encourage students to think for themselves and to organize information so that it has personal meaning. A simple example taken from the EQUALS Project in Berkeley, California, might help clarify this approach: "A school has 500 students. If a school bus holds 75 students, is there enough room on one bus for all the school's left-handed students?" The students are told that from 12% to 12½% of Americans are left-handed. Working in pairs, students are asked to solve the problem. Upon completion, each pair shares its solution with the class. Not surprisingly, a variety of solutions are produced.

The Interactive Mathematics Program developed by educators at San Francisco State University and the University of California at Berkeley is a complete high school mathematics curriculum. It is based on the principle that mathematics is best learned in the context of meaningful and interesting problems. Each of the four courses in the curriculum is organized around a central problem or theme. This organization enables students to integrate traditional mathematics content with new content in probability, statistics, sampling, curve-fitting, and linear programming. Students are grouped heterogenously for instruction. Much of the work is completed collaboratively in teams of four.

Several obvious benefits accrue from this approach to mathematics teaching: (1) Students learn to work together. (2) Students see the direct connection between mathematics and the real world. (3) Students learn from each other. (4) Artificial barriers among students and between groups of students are eliminated. (5) Technology, such as graphing calculators and personal computers, is used as a component of problem-solving strategies. (6) Students are asked to communicate their ideas in common parlance and in the language of mathematics. (7) Teachers facilitate student learning by asking challenging questions and clarifying individual and group thinking. (8) Assessment of student learning is aligned with instruction and the outcomes of the curriculum.

The role of the teacher in the new mathematics requires a break from traditional thinking. Teachers are less likely to provide right answers in an effort to challenge students to think for themselves. As the National Research Council states, "Teachers themselves need experience in doing mathematics—in exploring, guessing, testing, estimating, arguing, and proving. . . ." (National Research Council, 1989, p. 65) It is unlikely that many teachers will come to teaching with this background. It is, therefore, crucial that ongoing and consistent staff development be provided to help teachers acquire appropriate pedagogy and content. Like the students they hope to inspire, teachers are learners also. They must capture the spirit and the understanding of what is important for students to learn in order to create learning environments which acknowledge important differences within and among students.

SCIENCE

More than any other discipline, science teaching traditionally has paralleled the changes to instruction that are currently being recommended. Hands-on learning has dominated science labs. Individual projects were created by advanced students for science fairs and, in some cases, entry into the Westinghouse Talent Search. Community-based learning was offered to select students in professional labs or with university-based mentors.

Like its counterpart mathematics, science teaching was enhanced by the National Defense Education Act of the late 1950s. Inquiry-based learning was advocated in such projects as the Biological Sciences Curriculum Study (BSCS), Chem Study, and the Physical Science Study Curriculum (PSSC). Students were expected to delve into the structure of the discipline and to develop the "habits of mind" of the biologist, chemist, and physicist. Laboratory science was emphasized as students uncovered the mysteries of the sciences rather than simply covered the content of the textbook. Process science focused on the behaviors of observing, inferring, communicating, classifying, predicting, interpreting data, controlling variables, and formulating hypotheses. More enlightened teachers helped students to see that the processes could be transferred to aspects of every subject in the curriculum.

Today the emphasis is placed on active learning, problem-centered instruction, and hands-on experiences. Breadth of learning and conceptual understanding are valued more highly than content coverage which emphasizes facts, vocabulary, and recall. Students are expected to learn how to think and reason scientifically, experiment and test for truth, and reject hypotheses that cannot be supported by evidence. The difference between current expectations and the past seems best summarized by two statements: (1) *What was true for a few students is now crucial for all students.* (2) *Covering textbook material sequentially is out of step with the information and service demands of the society in which students are expected to take their places.*

Technological advances enable science teachers to facilitate student learning by offering high risk experiments without endangering students. When preparing an experiment on volcanoes, students can create an animated demonstration on a computer, as well as find video clips of famous eruptions such as Mount St. Helens. Animal dissections can be accomplished without bringing students in contact with specimens. Technology expands the eyes and ears of science. Probes and sensors can be used to alter variables in laboratory settings to test different effects. For example, pressure sensors allow students to study the rate of photosynthesis, and oxygen sensors allow for the study of oxygen consumption during plant and animal respiration. A new project, Image Processing for Teaching (IPT), allows students to create images by scanning or photographing objects with a digital or video camera. With image processing, students can analyze and enhance digital images to gain more information from the data. Scanners, video cameras, the Internet, and digital still cameras are used in conjunction with project activities (Raphael & Greenberg, 1995).

Students who have been unsuccessful with traditionally taught science find the new hands-on, minds-on approach more engaging. They learn to formulate hypotheses, organize and collect data, and write up the results. With teachers serving as coaches and facilitators, more students are exploring science by doing what scientists do. They participate in a scientific community focused on real-world problems. One high school student classified 2,000 volcanic edifices on Venus, and, working with a high school student in another state via e-mail, explored whether small volcanic edifices were associated with major geologic features on Venus. Historically, both students had poor records of achievement in science. Yet, when they were offered an opportunity to explore an area of interest in depth, they did so well that they were invited to give a presentation at NASA's annual Lunar and Planetary Science Conference.

HISTORY

Many a typical American history course ends with the teacher shouting, "We won World War II!," as the students leave the classroom for summer vacation. Unfortunately, the textbook approach still dominates most history teaching. Students are expected to learn history chronologically by memorizing names, dates, and key events. Teachers supplement and embellish the textbook content through presentations. The "sage on the stage" probably depicts the teacher of history better than any other discipline in the secondary school curriculum.

The new history standards call the strictly linear approach to history into question, urging new methodologies and the development of higher-level thinking for all students. "Their aim is to lead students to think more like historians—to formulate their own questions, learn the interpretive process, and develop new research skills" (ASCD, Winter, 1995, p.3). Primary source document kits are available from the National Archives on such topics as the Constitution, the Bill of Rights, and Westward Expansion. The Archives kits contain governmental records, family Bibles, birth and death certificates, and eyewitness accounts.

A number of history teachers have students begin investigations by asking questions about their family histories. By interviewing parents and relatives, students begin to reconstruct their own history and learn historical inquiry techniques in the process. The teacher facilitates the process. Students can also be encouraged to compare different accounts of the same historical event or check the authenticity of a historical novel or film.

History uniquely provides students with the opportunity to sift through different perspectives of an event and search for truth. By interviewing relatives and adult friends about a hurricane, election, or sporting event, students can learn that truth is often in the eye of the beholder. A trend toward including more contemporary events in the history curriculum enables the skillful teacher to help students see the historical antecedents in current affairs. For example, the concept of equality contains a rich collection of historical antecedents that can help students see with depth and perspective. Similar depth and breadth can be found in such themes as human rights, multiculturalism and change.

History, when taught well, usually displays four characteristics: (1) It emphasizes the human aspect of events. (2) It moves from the present to the past and back to the present in an ongoing dialectic. (3) It helps students to learn processes that historians use to investigate the past. (4) It shuns rote learning in favor of thinking and problem-solving.

GEOGRAPHY

Ostensibly, geography has been the stepchild of the secondary curriculum. Few, if any, secondary curricula include geography as a separate course. When it is included, it becomes what is called "pigs per acre" geography. Students are asked to memorize such meaningless facts as the climate or the major imports of various countries. The continents, major mountain ranges, and rivers are presented in the hope that students will be able to put the information together in some meaningful whole. This approach tends to make traditional courses in geography as unpopular as traditional courses in history.

A knowledge of geography seems critical to individual and collective success in today's world. Geography is the study of people, places, and environments, and an understanding and appreciation of those relationships. The new standards in geography call for students to be competent in knowledge and content and in performance, or "able to do" geography. The title of the standards document, *Geography for Life: National Standards* (1994), points to geography as a part of everyday life.

Students must create mental maps of the world so that they have a perspective of places and events on the globe. Television bombards students with events, places, and people from all over the world. Television also offers programs that can stimulate student interest in critical issues such as endangered species, acid rain, air and water pollution, and global warming. Geography builds on such experiences and focuses on cultures and environments different from one's own. It provides students with multiple opportunities for comparisons with their own life and lifestyle.

Problem-solving in geography can be accomplished singly, in pairs or in working groups. Students can even work with cohorts from other countries, learning about another culture in the process. Traditional teaching is replaced by "hands-on" activities and critical thinking. Students explore their own communities. They use primary and secondary sources to learn about how their communities operate and how they got that way. "They travel back in time to a fictional national park and map how they think things might change over time. . . . Students learn to inspect maps from different periods and analyze the changes in the natural landscape" (Dulli & Goodman, 1994).

Changes in instruction are facilitated by new materials. A picture atlas of the world on CD-ROM enhances teaching about countries. Multimedia materials from the National Geographic Society combine visual images, video clips, music, voice, and text to engage students' interest. The STV series of interactive videodisks brings together the Society's resources on the *Rain Forest* and a four volume series on *World Geography*. The accompanying software allows students to draw on the data bases to create their own presentations (Peterson, 1994).

THE ARTS

It is time to view the arts as essential learning in our postindustrial society. "The arts—from painting to poetry, from dancing to singing, from playing musical instruments to composing on synthesizers, from writing dialogue to acting in plays, from architecture to sculpture, from photography to pottery—should not be seen as merely pleasant diversions from the core academic basics of schools" (Sautter, 1994). Howard Gardner's work in multiple intelligences leads educators to consider music, art, and intrapersonal and interpersonal communications as aspects of human intelligence not tapped well by traditional school programs. It is Gardner's premise that there are at least seven different areas of intelligence. (Schools acknowledge only two.) The forgotten five include many characteristics associated with the arts.

In other counties it is assumed that all children can attain proficiency in the arts. The Suzuki method of teaching violin originated in the belief that ability is not inherited and can be improved through experience. All students in the Japanese system are expected to master one of the arts, usually a musical instrument. Student artists, whether dancers, musicians, writers, or actors, learn by doing. They experience their learning directly, learning from their mistakes. They develop a self-discipline which carries over into other aspects of their lives. Mastering one of the art forms is often a lifetime commitment that transcends course completion and the accumulation of credits.

The prevailing approach to art education is discipline-based, in art production, art history, and art criticism. Its aim is to enable all youngsters, whatever their innate abilities, to acquire the skills, knowledge, and attitudes appropriate for making or encountering works of art as an educated adult" (Day, Eisner, Stake, Wilson, & Wilson, 1984, p.3). Art is learning a different way of knowing reality. Students who experience the arts emerge with an enhanced perspective from which to resolve problems and enjoy life.

Teaching the arts means more than simply teaching students a variety of techniques. While technique is important, the ability to analyze the compositions of various painters, composers, lyricists, and writers enables novice artists to explore possibilities for their own works. In this sense, the arts are a vehicle for self-expression and an opportunity to compare one's own values with others. Our students must learn to live and work in a culturally diverse country and world. By probing below the surface of music and the visual arts, an insightful teacher can assist students to resonate across cultural barriers.

Technology has also come to instruction in the arts through synthesizers and CD-ROMs. Electronics can aid in music composition and editing, and in combining music and images to illustrate nuances of a composer's intent. Laser disks bring art galleries to schools without students ever leaving the premises. They can also store the complete works of Shakespeare, Whitman, Bach, and Frank Lloyd Wright for easy and quick access. In some states, instrumental music teachers are able to listen to, critique, and advise students in another part of the state through satellite television and telephone. Equipment to produce CDs will soon be available at a reasonable cost to enable students to create their own portfolios of music, art, dance, and dramatic performances.

TESTING AND INSTRUCTION

Assessment is an essential ingredient for the improvement of instruction. If instruction is the means by which standards and outcomes are delivered to students, then assessment measures the degree to which the standards and outcomes have been achieved. Assessment and testing are often used interchangeably. Tests, however, are only one form of assessment. Assessment goes beyond testing and includes such activities as demonstrations, oral and written presentations, recitals, performances, contests, projects, and individual and group problem-solving. Athletic competitions are assessments of how well a team or an individual has prepared for a contest. How a team or individual plays may also assess the quality of coaching and the talent and motivation of the participants. A dramatic performance is an assessment of the cast's talents and readiness. The audience response is a measure of the quality of the performance.

In all cases, the method of assessment should fit the purpose of instruction. If students are expected to learn to write well, the competency can hardly be measured by multiple choice questions about grammar. Having the students write or develop responses to open-ended questions would seem a more suitable device. Correspondingly, writing across the curriculum emphasizes the importance of good writing in a variety of contexts and is appropriately measured by the teachers of the specific disciplines.

Curriculum standards or goals establish targets for instruction and assessment. Assuming that the new nationally focused standards are valid, assessment of the achievement of these goals also assesses the efficacy of the instructional process. As English (1992) points out, pertinent assessment should measure pupil attainment in relationship to outcome indicators. Nothing less is acceptable. Tests or other forms of student assessment must align with outcome indicators if the results are to serve as useful measures of student learning.

Most teachers and administrators are poorly prepared in assessment. Few states require competence in assessment as a condition of licensing. Increasing recognition of the importance of assessment, however, argues for administrative and teacher grounding in the basics of its techniques and processes. Currently, a collaborative project of the American Association of School Administrators, the National Association of Elementary Principals, the National Association of Secondary School Principals, and the National Council for Measurement in Education has begun to address the need for administrators to become assessment literate. A new report on high school restructuring jointly sponsored by the Carnegie Foundation for the Advancement of Teaching and the National Association of Secondary School Principals, *Breaking Ranks* (1996), also contains several recommendations linking assessment practices to instructional reform and identifies the principal as the key person to accept the mantle of assessment leadership.

Richard Stiggins (1995) contends that, "assessment literates know the difference between sound and unsound assessment. . . . (They) come to assessment knowing what they are assessing, why they are doing so, how best to assess the achievement of interest, how to generate sound samples of performance, what can go wrong, and how to prevent those problems before they occur" (p. 240). They also never place students in situations where their achievement might be mismeasured. Principals, as instructional leaders, are in a unique position to construct and promote a new vision of the assessment process. They can help teachers see that good teaching and good assessment go hand in glove.

NEW FORMS OF ASSESSMENT

The new standards developed by professional groups in mathematics, English/language arts, science, history, and geography emphasize that students must acquire the capabilities to deal with problems, analyze and interpret data, think critically, formulate questions, and complete extended projects singly and in cooperative groups. The SCANS Report (1991) concluded that the qualities associated with high performance in most competitive companies should guide the development of standards for all schooling; that schools must be retooled into high performance organizations, preparing students to be successful adults; and that students must develop a new set of competencies and foundation skills to become successful adults in this economy. The necessary competencies include creative thinking, decision-making, problem-solving, and reasoning.

Technological advances now make it possible for students to interact directly with primary sources. No longer are students sheltered from real-world experiences by parents or parent surrogates. Students more and more must act upon their experiences and construct their own meanings. These conditions promise to become even more pronounced as the 21st century approaches. Traditional forms of instruction and assessment will not succeed in supporting these new conditions. What is needed is a closer link between instruction and assessment, one in which assessment tasks resemble learning tasks. New goals require a more diverse kind of teaching if all students are to be successful. New goals and teaching also require new forms of assessment—an authentic assessment.

The concept of *alternative assessment* encompasses a variety of ways to measure student learning. The choices of assessment should be consistent with the purposes of instruction. If the purpose of instruction is to help students acquire content knowledge, one form of assessment may be used. If the purpose is to have students apply knowledge in the solution of real-world problems, then another form of assessment will surely be appropriate. No single assessment can meet all instructional needs. The cloth should be cut to fit the wearer.

In Chapter 4, we discussed the importance of authentic instruction and assessment. Authentic assessments focus on real-life situations. They emphasize the application of knowledge and skills in the real (or simulated) contexts in which the knowledge and skills are actually used. Probably the two best known forms of authentic assessment are portfolios and performance assessment.

Portfolio assessment emphasizes problem-solving, reasoning, effective written communication, and research skills while still allowing the assessment of knowledge and the comprehension of facts, concepts, and procedures. It is a comprehensive assessment of student understanding. Portfolios are more than open folders into which selected samples of student work are filed for future reference. They are structured to contain specific kinds of samples of student work consistent with curriculum goals and instructional objectives. A well-crafted portfolio includes a table of contents, five to seven pieces of student work germane to the subject or topic, and written justification from the student for selecting each piece of work. A portfolio concurrently assesses student performance and helps the student internalize standards of quality.

Quality is a topic that is rarely discussed with students. Most teachers seem to think that students know what quality work is. Unfortunately, this is usually not the case. If the adage that students get good at what they spend time doing is correct, then ample time must be devoted to helping them understand the concept of quality. Teachers should begin the process by talking about quality in a general way. The general discussion might focus on the things in the students' world that they judge to be of quality and why. For example, they might begin by asking students to look for quality in how they dress, how they wear their hair, their music, and the movies they attend. The discussions do not have to be long, just frequent. Subsequently, teachers can engage students in discussions about the meaning of quality applied to the subjects or topics under study and then to the nature of their own work.

Performance assessments are skill tests that students complete in the context of instruction. They measure a student's ability to perform tasks such as essays, speeches, playing a musical instrument, driving a car, or conducting a science experiment. Anyone who ever participated in scouting will remember the procedures for earning a merit badge. The required outcome was described in the merit badge book. When the scout was ready to be tested, he or she performed the required behavior. For example, if a scout wanted to receive a merit badge in international Morse code, he or she learned the code and then practiced until the required skill level was reached. This procedure is similar to performance-based instruction. The final performances in this approach are described at the beginning of instruction so that students know what is expected of them. Instruction is then varied to meet the learning needs of different students. Time is varied and under the control of the student and the teacher(s). Students decide when they are ready to complete the final assessment. The final assessment rates the successful completion of the outcome, or provides data for retaining the students until the outcome is mastered.

The evaluation of a performance outcome requires valid and reliable criteria for determining quality. Criteria are established as scoring rubrics and applied to students' work. Ryan and Miyasaka (1995) offer a modified approach to rubrics adapted from the work of Marzano, Pickering, and McTighe. Four basic approaches to rating student performances are listed: holistic, modified holistic, modified analytic, and analytic. The *holistic* approach compares the student performance to a series of models and rates it based on the model it most closely resembles. The *modified holistic* approach assigns a score to the student's performance based on the teacher's judgment of the work on a scale with defined levels of performance. The *modified analytic* approach assigns a partial score based on the teacher's judgment of specific learning dimensions underlying the student's performance. For each learning dimension, particular levels of performance are defined with the number of points to be awarded. These points are summed for a total score of performance. In the *analytic* approach, the specific characteristics of the performance are thought to be of greater importance than the total. Each of several learning dimensions is defined along with the number of points to be awarded.

These scoring rubrics move from the general to the specific. The more analytic the feedback, the more diagnostic and helpful to students in improving and refining their performance. As students become more acclimated to the concept of scoring rubrics, they can be taught to design their own. Like the process described for portfolios, students in time can become skillful in evaluating the quality of their own work and the work of others. Self-appraisal is a characteristic often associated with creative people and one that leads to pride in workmanship.

Assessment should be continuous to determine the effectiveness of instruction and instructional plans. Gathering salient information on an ongoing basis enables teachers to make adjustments in the instructional process. If schools are to serve all students well, and if success for all students is a goal, then continuous adjustments in instruction are needed. As W. Edwards Deming observed, "The right time for attention to final outcomes in any production process, including the learning process, is every step of the way."

Assessment is integral and essential to good instruction. Teachers must be helped to understand the importance of this relationship. The objectives of instruction serve as beginning points for constructing appropriate assessment instruments. Various kinds may be needed. When using performance-based assessment, for example, teachers must learn how to develop scoring mechanisms for judging quality. Scoring rubrics are really criteria for judging the quality of student performance. Teachers can create scoring rubrics for various activities by working in pairs, or in study groups of five to seven. Once teachers master the concept of scoring rubrics, study groups might continue with materials such as Richard Stiggin's *Student Centered Classroom Assessment* (1995), Robert Marzano, et al.'s *Assessing Student Outcomes: Performance Assessment Using the Dimensions of Learning Model* (1993), or Grant Wiggins' *Assessing Student Performance* (1993).

School-based decision making is a strong current trend. Carried to its ultimate implementation, local decision making means local control of curriculum, instruction, and assessment. When these three important dimensions constitute a functioning system, school improvement and accountability are possible. Accountability also can be strengthened by action research, which is a systematic way to improve school practices. (See Chapter 9.)

ACTION STEPS

◆ Visit a middle or high school. Obtain permission to photograph instruction in classrooms or learning environments where English/language arts, social studies, the arts, or mathematics are offered. What instructional strategies appear to be specific to the subject? What strategies appear general in nature? What tentative conclusions can be drawn from the observations? Present the findings in a slide presentation to a group of middle or high school educators.

◆ Investigate one of the subject matter projects referenced in this chapter, such as writing across the curriculum, the EQUALS Project, primary source kits from the National Archives, materials from the National Geographic Society, and the Arts Propel. What kind of instruction is advocated? How could the project be introduced to appropriate faculty to encourage consideration?

◆ Review test items contained in the *National Assessment of Student Progress*. How can items such as these be used to help teachers create assessment devices more aligned with authentic pedagogy?

◆ Develop a staff development program designed to help teachers learn about new forms of assessment. Include activities in writing standards and benchmarks which reflect problem-solving and the application of knowledge. Create assessment activities to measure the attainment of both.

7

SCHEDULING AND INSTRUCTIONAL ORGANIZATION

The purpose of a school schedule is to assign teachers and students to courses and classrooms during the school day. Typically, a school schedule has been defined as six or seven periods of equal lengths of time with additional time for passing and lunch. The traditional school schedule is a product of the factory model, and the traditional school year reflects an agrarian mindset. Western civilizations think in terms of monochromatic time, i.e., one thing is done at a time. Classes are separate entities. Teaching is accomplished in classrooms by teachers working alone.

The concept of monochromatic time impacts how curriculum is conceived and how instruction is delivered. Events are seen as separate from other events. The coverage of knowledge and skills must precede any concern for real-world problems. This condition makes it difficult for teachers and parents to rationalize the use of teaching methods such as cooperative learning. (Some parents view cooperative learning as detrimental to abler students.) But monochromatic time is a matter of perspective. Inhabitants of Eastern cultures see time differently. They believe that all events happen simultaneously. It is what people focus on that makes them appear as separate. All events arise from a common origin.

Since the late 1950s people have gradually become more identity conscious. As electronic communication systems have expanded, there has been a corresponding turn inward for the individual. Marshall McLuhan observed that the placement of satellites in space was akin to surrounding the earth with our central nervous system, thus causing people to become more introspective. His global village was a description of the interconnectedness of all life caused by the technological revolution. Events occurring on one part of the globe were known instantaneously on other parts of the globe. Quantum physics was becoming a reality right in front of the television set.

Historical Perspective

The 1960s brought a period of inquiry and innovation in education. Innovations like nongraded schools and continuous progress education were introduced. A search began for school schedules that offered more options for students and teachers. There was much interest in flexible scheduling. Modular-flexible schedules were attempted in many high schools to provide different timeframes for different activities. Some activities seemed to require longer than the typical 50- to 55-minute period, while some required less time. The six-period day was reconceptualized in these schools to one with 15 to 30 short modules. Modules of 15, 20, 25, and 30 minutes replaced the conventional class period. Teachers requested *"mods"* depending on the activities planned. A chemistry lab might require 2 hours (eight 15-minute mods), while a chemistry lecture only needed 30 to 60 minutes. Courses were scheduled for different lengths of time on different days of the week. Table 7.1 (on pages 122–123) is a sample modular schedule.

The variety of choices in time patterns was unlimited. It was the responsibility of the administration and teachers to make appropriate changes throughout the school year. In theory, a student's schedule could change as the planned activities for given subjects changed. The idea was to fit the time pattern to the planned learning activity. The sample shows a longer time frame for a biology lab, meeting 2 days of 6, and three meetings of physical education. The blank spaces were unscheduled time when students were able to use the library, confer with a teacher or a counselor, study, or go to an open lab for additional work in a subject. Unfortunately, unscheduled time became an albatross when many students chose to sit in the corridors and socialize.

In many cases, once the modular schedule was in place, it developed a kind of rigidity. Time patterns remained stable; days looked the same throughout the school year. Special events such as field trips and assemblies were treated as they would be in traditionally scheduled schools and were superimposed over the master schedule.

Some schedules allowed for large group, small group, and independent study activities. In the NASSP Model Schools Project (1969–74) students were scheduled into large group motivational sessions and followup small group discussions in each of eight or nine subjects areas on a regular basis. Large group classes of 100 or more students in a given subject area were scheduled for two 20-minute modules. Seminar-size groups of 15 or fewer students met following the large group presentations to discuss the content of the large groups and to clarify students' thinking. Sometimes the followup groups were on different days of the week. Independent study in each subject was scheduled the remainder of the time. Students worked on study guides, learning activity packages, or UNIPAKS under the supervision of a teacher or a paraprofessional. Resources to complete the work were housed in the study areas. Independent study was scheduled for two, three, four, or more modules on different days of the week. Thus, a student would attend four to eight large group sessions per week, four to eight small-group seminars, and several hours of independent study. Much of a student's week was spent working on materials at his or her own pace.

Schedules in the Model Schools Project were fairly rigid for large and small group instruction, but quite flexible when it came to independent study. Each student had a teacher adviser who helped create the advisee's schedule, monitored progress and was empowered to change the amount of independent study accordingly. In a given week, a student typically devoted 65–75% of his or her time to independent study. Students who demonstrated an inability to handle independent study were

TABLE 7.1. STUDENT MODULAR SCHEDULE FOR A 6-DAY CYCLE

Module	Day 1	Day 2	Day 3	Day 4	Day 5	Day 6
1	English 10 →		Am. History →	Biology →	Spanish II →	
2		Geometry →				English 10 →
3						
4						
5		Spanish II →		Am. History →	Biology →	Geometry →
6						
7	Geometry →		English 10 →	Geometry →		P.E.
8						
9					Biology Lab →	
10		Lunch				
11	Spanish II					

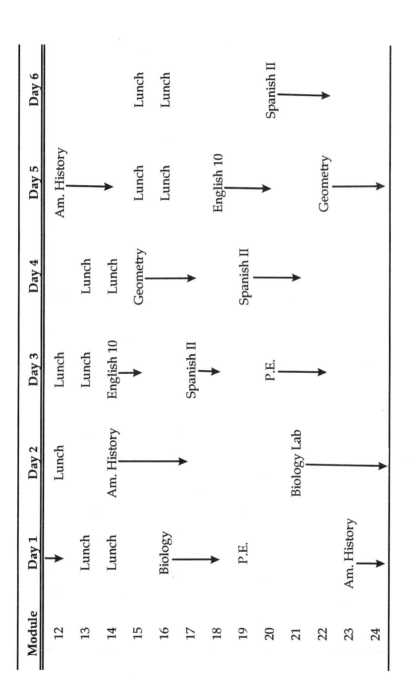

Module	Day 1	Day 2	Day 3	Day 4	Day 5	Day 6
12	→	Lunch	Lunch		Am. History →	
13	Lunch		Lunch	Lunch		Lunch
14	Lunch	Am. History →	English 10 →	Lunch		Lunch
15	Biology			Geometry →	Lunch	
16					Lunch	
17	→		Spanish II →			
18				Spanish II →	English 10 →	
19	P.E.					
20			P.E. →			Spanish II →
21		Biology Lab				
22		→			Geometry →	
23	Am. History →					
24					→	

assigned a modified traditional schedule. Teachers also had flexible schedules which enabled them to find time for conferring with students, working with advisees and planning instruction.

In nongraded high schools of the 1960s, there were two major approaches to scheduling. The first approach organized curriculum by phases which were defined as temporary stages in a student's intellectual development. Phase one courses were for students with serious deficiencies. Phase two courses targeted students with some deficiencies. Phase three courses were for students with average achievement. Phase four students studied a subject in depth. Phase five courses were college level in scope. In building the schedule, care was taken to arrange as many phases during a class period as possible. This arrangement allowed students to move upward or downward in a subject as their progress indicated. Students were individually scheduled by diagnosed achievement levels in the major disciplines. Thus a student could be phase one in one subject, phase two in two others, and phase three in the rest. Typical time patterns were a six-period day with some extended blocks of time on alternate days of the week.

The second approach to the nongraded high school was called continuous progress. Curricula were sequenced from basic concepts and skills to more sophisticated ones. Learning packages were developed by teachers for each concept and/or skill. Students were placed in the continuum on the basis of a pretest and previous achievement in the subject. Their progress was individual and largely under their control. Science, for example, might be organized by concepts rather than the traditional sequence of physical science, biology, chemistry and physics. In one high school, science contained 50 sequences that students completed at their own pace. When students completed all 50, they were encouraged to enroll in more advanced work. A modified flexible-modular schedule was the typical vehicle for continuous progress. Many of the schools in the NASSP Model Schools Project utilized this approach, but schedules were easy to change because of teacher adviser involvement.

Several important considerations were embedded in the scheduling efforts of educators during the 1960s. Time was primarily seen as a variable and not a constant. Time only measured contact, not student achievement. The length of time students were scheduled for a learning activity was based on what seemed necessary to complete the activity. Uniform time periods were rare and replaced by a philosophy that fitted time and place to the learning task. Additionally, teachers and students took part in the scheduling process. In some cases, arena scheduling was implemented to give students an opportunity to select their teachers and meeting days and times. Likewise, teachers accepted or rejected students based on optimal class size, achievement, and perceived motivation. Bell schedules were frequently eliminated except to announce the beginning and the end of the school day. The individual student was paramount. Student needs were instrumental in determining appropriate curricula, appropriate time arrangements, and appropriate instructional strategies.

Current Efforts at Schedule Reform

Contemporary efforts to restructure schools have generated a renewed interest in changing the school schedule. The most popular approach is the block schedule in which students take fewer courses for longer periods of time. This notion was also popular in the 1960s, but primarily in junior high and middle schools (which were just getting started). The block schedule typically combined instruction in two subjects that supported each other. In the Dade County, Florida, schools, basic education was a term given to combined English and social studies at the junior high level. Another approach assigned a group of students to an interdisciplinary team of teachers for a block of time. The team rescheduled students within the block based on common instructional planning and subject demands.

Today block scheduling can be found in many high schools. One approach is the Copernican Plan advanced by Joseph Carroll, a former superintendent in New Mexico and Massachusetts. It is Carroll's belief that time constraints imposed by the Carnegie unit are *the* major impediment to sound high school reform. He cites as evidence that summer programs where students are able to concentrate on one or two subjects are superior to the traditional system of six subjects taken each semester. In the Copernican system, students take fewer subjects for longer periods of time. Blocks of 90, 120, or 240 minutes are scheduled each day. Students are able to focus their time and teachers get to know the students better. Teachers have fewer preparations and fewer students.

Block scheduling may vary. One simple approach is a six-period day and double periods 4 days per week. Periods 1, 3, and 5 meet for a double period on Mondays and Wednesdays, and periods 2, 4, and 6 have a double period on Tuesdays and Thursdays. All six classes meet for a single period on Fridays. A variation of this schedule doubles the periods over a 2-week cycle so that every class meets for two periods 5 of every 10 days.

Another variation on earlier block schedules offers a seven-period day on a rotational basis, doubling one class period per week. Classes meet for the same number of minutes during the week, but do not meet each day. The rotational schedule also caters, in part, to individual time of day preferences and differing time-related energy levels. Table 7.2 shows the movement of class periods throughout the week so that each day is slightly different. The double-class meetings allow teachers to plan longer activities.

The four-by-four model of block scheduling enrolls students in only four courses each semester. Extending class periods to 85 or 95 minutes enables students to complete a year's work in a semester and eight courses per year. Two variations of the four-by-four schedule are shown in Tables 7.3 and 7.4. Advanced placement courses may be a problem for this schedule since the AP examinations are not given until the spring. As a result, some schools still schedule advanced placement courses on a yearly rather than a semester basis.

In the four-by-four schedule, students take only four classes each semester (90 days). Teachers teach three classes per semester with no more than 90 students, and have an 85 to 95-minute planning period. The additional planning time enables teachers to teach six classes per year rather than the five in more traditional schedules. The fact that teachers teach fewer students per semester also provides them with the opportunity to plan more personalized programs.

TABLE 7.2. A ROTATIONAL SCHEDULE WITH DOUBLE PERIODS

Time	Monday	Tuesday	Wednesday	Thursday	Friday
8:00	1	7	6	5	3
9:00	2	1	7	6	5
10:00	2	1	7	6	5
11:00	3	2	1	7	6
12:00	4	4	4	4	4
1:30	5	3	2	3	7
2:30	6	3	5	2	1

* Period 4 includes lunch

TABLE 7.3. A BLOCK SCHEDULE WITH A LUNCH, ACTIVITIES, AND A STUDY HALL PERIOD

7:55–9:10	First Block
9:15–10:40	Second Block
10:45–11:40	Lunch, Activities, Study Hall
11:45–1:10	Third Block
1:15–2:40	Fourth Block

TABLE 7.4. A BLOCK SCHEDULE WITH A COMMON LUNCH PERIOD

8:15–9:45	First Block
9:50–11:25	Second Block
11:30–12:15	Lunch
12:20–1:50	Third Block
1:55–3:30	Fourth Block

Still another variation of the block schedule comes from the Coalition of Essential Schools. In his book, *Horace's School: Redesigning the American High School*, Ted Sizer (1992) proposes a sample high school schedule designed to tailor school practices to the needs of every group of adolescents (Table 7.5). Periods 1, 2, and 6 are 1-hour and 45 minutes each. Periods 3, 4, and 5 share 2 hours for lunch, advisory, and tutorials by the teaching team. Team members decide on group and individual activities. Tutorials are scheduled for individual students by advisers. Period 1 has a 10-minute passing period; all others have 5 minutes. Subjects are scheduled on a 4-day rotation to provide opportunities for teachers and students to meet at different times of the day.

TABLE 7.5. SAMPLE SCHEDULE FROM THE COALITION OF ESSENTIAL SCHOOLS

Time	Monday	Tuesday	Wednesday	Thursday	Friday
7:00–8:00	Activities (band, chorus, etc.)				
8:00–9:45	Period 1				
9:55–11:45	Period 2				
11:45–1:45	Periods 3, 4, and 5: Lunch, Advisory, Tutorials				
1:45–3:30	Period 6				
3:30–4:00	Team Meetings for the Staff				
4:00	Activities (band, chorus, etc.)				

The longer time periods permit students to take part in community service and other extended experiences. Teachers have time to plan with colleagues, to serve as advisers to a prescribed number of students, to work on curriculum, instruction and assessment, and to contact parents. These priorities show the relationship of scheduling to the purposes of the school. The schedule is a key ingredient in helping a school staff achieve the school's goals and objectives. One justification often presented for block scheduling is that it forces teachers to consider other approaches to instruction than traditional lecture, discussion, or direct approaches. Such thinking clearly places the educational cart before the horse. The schedule should grow out of the philosophical and pedagogical assumptions defined and held by the school staff.

ASSUMPTIONS AND GUIDELINES FOR SCHEDULING

The number of days and hours that schools operate is usually fixed by state statute. How the days and time are used, however, is limited only by the creativity of the school leadership. The following assumptions and beliefs about teaching and learning can serve as a basis for changing a school schedule, both in terms of what students and teachers do and the time with which they have to do it.

♦ Students bring different knowledge, skills and learning styles to the school.

♦ Students should complete learning tasks in the best setting for the work to be completed.

♦ Engaged time is related to the intrinsic motivation that individual students bring to a learning activity.

♦ In-depth learning experiences often require longer time periods than traditional schedules provide.

♦ Teachers need time to plan instruction, meet with colleagues, confer with advisees, develop assessment devices, and participate in professional development activities.

- Credit for learning should be based on what students can do and not on the amount of time spent.
- The size of an instructional group should depend on the activity to be completed.
- Decisions about time and learning are best made by those closest to the act of learning, the teachers and the students.

A STUDENT-DRIVEN SCHEDULE

Since students and teachers are most directly affected by the school schedule, how might a schedule be created which optimally serves both parties? The ideal schedule would adapt to the needs of each student and each teacher. Several of the schedules previously discussed suggest the initial steps in the process. With the present state-of-the-art computer technology, it is possible to produce a personalized schedule for each student and a professionally satisfying schedule for each teacher.

A personalized approach to scheduling would provide alternatives to placing all students and teachers in classrooms for uniform periods of time. Ostensibly, one could begin with a blank sheet. Teachers and students could fill in the blanks by requesting times for specific activities. In some cases, special groups would be necessary. Band and chorus are two such activities. Seminars or small-group discussions, teacher presentations of content, and similar activities require specific places and time periods. Any activity that could only be accomplished by a group or whose objectives were better achieved by meeting in groups could be placed on the blank schedule. Since some meetings would be ongoing while others would be transitory, the master schedule would change as activities necessitated group changes.

Two ingredients seem necessary to the development of a more personalized school schedule for students. Both students and teachers need input into the use of time. Teachers can accomplish this by making requests through team leaders or department chairs or other representatives. A broad-based scheduling committee could collect information from teachers and modify the schedule accordingly. This information would be communicated to teacher advisers who would meet with individual students to guide their scheduling decisions. Student involvement could be accomplished through the advisers who would approve scheduling decisions and monitor individual student progress.

Students would spend a fair amount of time working independently, in triads or pairs or in problem-solving groups, in topic-study, or apprenticeship clusters. These arrangements would require a reconceptualizing of curriculum and instruction. Obviously, state and local mandates must be acknowledged, such as graduation requirements, length of the school day, and minutes per subject per week. Waiver processes are now in effect in most states that permit some latitude in redefining credits and time. Performance-based learning seems a viable alternative to extant requirements. Placing the emphasis on performance rather than time increases the opportunities for student choices in curriculum and instruction.

Continuous progress education is one approach to performance-based learning that simultaneously personalizes the instructional process. General outcomes are identified for each subject in the curriculum, or by courses within subjects. Interdisciplinary or project approaches can be created. Units of instruction are developed around clusters of objectives and materials, permitting students or cohorts to progress at their own pace. Further personalization can take place when instructional options account for different student learning styles and different student interests. When students complete all the units or topics associated with a course and demonstrate mastery of the objectives, they advance in the sequence. In continuous progress programs, students are able to complete unit and course assessments when they are ready to do so.

Figure 7.1 provides a schematic of a learning sequence organized for continuous progress.

FIGURE 7.1. SCHEMATIC OF A CONTINUOUS PROGRESS LEARNING SEQUENCE

Course

Unit   Unit   Unit   Unit   Unit   Unit   Unit   Unit   Unit   Unit   Unit   Unit

---

The twelve units are organized around the essential outcomes of the course. Each unit is designed to help students achieve specific outcomes. A variety of learning activities are created to assist students in achieving the outcomes. The learning activities may include reading textbooks, other reading materials, interactive technology, seminars, experiments, projects, community-based learning experiences or hands-on materials. They are designed to accommodate individual student learning styles and knowledge level. Assessments are aligned with the unit outcomes.

Contracting is another way to personalize the learning process. Contracting can be integrated into a continuous progress system, or it can stand alone. With contracting, students design their own learning environments with the help of teachers. Contracts contain objectives, activities and planned ways to assess performance. A completion schedule is developed to facilitate monitoring by the student and the teachers. The flexibility of contracting allows individual students to focus on different objectives and content while simultaneously adjusting for learning style. A typical contract is a formalized, written document that specifies the objectives, the content, the proposed learning activities, a list of resources, a timeline with due dates, and a method of assessment. It also contains a signature section for the student, the teacher, the adviser, and the parents.

Contract learning places major responsibility for directing and executing learning upon the student. Hence, it is wise to include student training. The training program can gradually induct students into the process. Initially teachers may wish to assume a coaching responsibility for selecting and organizing content, developing activities and assigning due dates. Gradually students will be able to create their own structures. Some students are obviously more prepared than others for taking responsibility.

Students contract to complete various parts of a course or a project. The task is made easier when the objectives are described by outcomes rather than by content or textbook chapters. All parties who sign the contract are responsible for monitoring progress. Since contracting deeply involves the students in the process of directing their own learning, it tends to build motivation intrinsic to the learning task.

The unit format and contracting lend themselves to a more personalized approach to scheduling. Much student work is completed solo or with a few other students. Aside from required group meetings, supervised or independent study comprises much of a student's daily, weekly and yearly schedule. Figure 7.2 shows a sample student-driven schedule from the Thomas Haney Secondary Centre in Maple Ridge, British Columbia.

In this schedule, fixed times are established for choir, self-defense class, and advisement group. All other times are arranged between the student and the teacher adviser. Students meet with their advisory group once per week, check in with their advisers each morning for attendance purposes, and schedule individual meetings as needed. Teacher-scheduled meetings for seminars, videos, guest speakers, or debates are arranged on a weekly basis and e-mailed to advisers. Students affected by group meetings place the meeting on their individual schedules. Advisers monitor student progress and the time each student devotes to the study of the various subjects. Advances in technology will soon permit students using laptop computers to download their daily and weekly schedules into a larger computer to control for the numbers of students selecting any one space at the same time. At Thomas Haney, students usually enroll in four to five courses at a time. When they complete a course, they choose a new one with the assistance of their adviser and professional counselor.

The consumer-driven schedule offers more flexibility for teachers. Working in teams, teachers develop units, create contracts, plan presentations, lead seminars, arrange for computer use, work with individual students, advise, analyze assessments of student performance, complete action research projects, and a host of

FIGURE 7.2. STUDENT-DRIVEN PERSONALIZED SCHEDULE

Monday:

8:30–9:30	Advisement
9:30–10:30	Self-defense class (small gym)
10:30–12:00	Choir
12:00–1:00	Lunch and media center work
1:00–2:00	Start work on short story unit for English
2:00–3:00	Continue working on social studies unit on revolution

Tuesday:

8:30–9:30	English seminar, room 1127
9:30–10:30	Self-defense class (small gym)
10:30–11:00	Continue working on contract for French, "Moi"
11:00–12:00	Continue working on short story unit
12:00–1:00	Lunch and media center work
1:00–2:00	Continue working on revolution unit
2:00–3:00	View video, social studies (media center)

Wednesday:

8:30–10:30	Continue working on French contract
10:30–12:00	Choir
12:00–1:00	Lunch and meet with adviser
1:00–2:00	Continue working on short story unit
2:00–3:00	Continue working on revolution unit

Thursday:

8:30–9:30	Advisement group
9:30–10:30	Self-defense (small gym)
10:30–12:00	Continue working on short story unit; Prepare for test
12:00–1:00	Lunch and media center work
1:00–2:00	Continue working on revolution unit; Prepare for debate
2:00–3:00	Continue working on French contract; Audiotape dialogue

Friday:

8:30–9:30	English test, short story (testing center)
9:30–10:30	Present dialogue tape to French teacher; Listen together and critique
10:30–12:00	Continue working on social studies debate; Meet with other students
12:00–1:00	Lunch and meeting with counselor
1:00–3:00	Social studies debate (Downtown Civic Center)

other professional activities. They do not meet with classes of 25–30 students in typical classrooms. Classroom spaces are replaced by project and resource areas where students can work with a variety of materials focused on one or more subjects or topics.

Cognitive apprenticeships may require additional variations in the personalized schedule, but the basic assumptions, guidelines, and instructional processes still hold. Teachers model the target outcomes or performances and coach their students. In Topic Study, for example, the process begins with a story or narrative read by the teacher, followed by in-depth analysis in small groups. Activities flow out of the discussion which may take several weeks if supplementary reading and research are needed. Emphasis is placed on exploration of ideas, hypothesis generation, problem-solving, and teaching for comprehension. Students work with the teacher acting as coach and with each other in small groups, or independently with interactive software, to pursue content related to the topic and to produce written and diagrammatic reports that thoroughly characterize the concepts and dimensions of the topic. Products include written reports, essays, diaries, poems, stories, and computer programs (Farnham-Diggory, 1992).

Scheduling for cognitive apprenticeships will require flexible use of time and the availability of teachers who can assume the dual role of subject matter coaches and academic advisers. Both continuous progress arrangements and contracting can facilitate apprenticeships, but a project or cohort approach may be more convenient if much of the activity requires small group work. In this case, a flexible block schedule may be the vehicle of choice. A four-by-four schedule or other extended block-of-time schedule ("pontoon," "fluid block") may better serve this form of pedagogy.

ORGANIZATION OF THE LEARNING ENVIRONMENT

The term learning environment is infinitely more appropriate than classroom to describe the new contingencies in American education. Given the expanded goals and objectives for education, the classroom with one teacher and 30 students is much too limiting. While the concept of a learning environment could include a classroom, it is much more. The exterior walls of the school now join it with the outside world rather than separate it. Technology places learners in touch with a universe of knowledge from which they can construct their own meanings. The learning environment is everywhere. Helping students make sense of expanding knowledge and conflicting values takes precedence over transmitting fixed bodies of information. The information highway is replete with opportunities for learning. Schools must prepare students to use them advantageously.

The school building and its main components are part of the learning environment. The human and nonhuman resources must be used effectively if all students are to learn. How these resources are deployed is the responsibility of the principal and the leadership team. A management/design team comprised of administrators and key teachers becomes the major decision-making body at the school. They help establish the school mission and vision, its major assumptions, and common student outcomes. They work to create a school learning organization. They propose staffing patterns, the design of the curriculum, the use of the facilities, staff development, budgeting, the school schedule, and the school action plan. Since the school is a team, it is common for the management team to involve various school personnel in planning the implementation strategies in several of these areas.

In a school committed to success for all students, a personalized approach to school organization is critical. What students do, where and with whom they do it, and for what length of time are all part of the personalized equation. Students also need someone at the school who knows them well enough to guide such decisions. That person is a teacher adviser. The teacher adviser is a professional staff member who devotes substantial time (2–5 hours) each week to help students become entrepreneurs of their own education. When all professional staff members participate directly, an adviser-advisee ratio of approximately 15:1 is possible. The lower the number of advisees per adviser, the more likely that students will be known well by at least one professional on the school staff.

Advisees meet with their teacher adviser on a regular basis. They check in with the adviser each morning for attendance purposes, but the grist of the relationship is found in one-to-one conferences where individual schedules are created and academic progress is discussed. The development of daily and weekly schedules is initiated in the advisory group and refined during individual conferences. The teacher adviser helps the student manage time effectively.

Organizing the faculty into disciplinary or interdisciplinary teams builds on the strengths of the teachers. Like students, teachers have individual strengths, talents and interests. When departments are organized into teams with appointed or elected team leaders, these individual differences can be used to strengthen instructional programs for all students. Teaming allows for more students to experience the best a faculty has to offer. Some teachers are best at presenting information in a dynamic and interesting way. Why shouldn't all students be the beneficiaries? Some teachers are expert at conducting open-ended seminars? Their questioning strategies help groups of students probe deeply into subject matter. Their ability to put students at ease invites all students to participate. Why shouldn't all students benefit? Some teachers create imaginative instructional materials which address the learning needs of all students. Why shouldn't all teachers in a department or a division benefit from their talents? Some teachers are great coaches. They know how to get the best performance from their students. Why shouldn't all students benefit? Students needing remedial help in a content area or in general learning skills can be accommodated when teachers work in teams. A cognitive skills resource teacher, for example, operates much like a reading resource teacher by offering special "skills shops" to needy students two to three times per week.

The interests and talents of teachers constitute one way to differentiate responsibility in a school. Another way to differentiate a staff is to add paraprofessionals, volunteers and student teachers. Hiring fewer teachers and redeploying the dollars to hire clerical assistants, general aides, and instructional assistants provides additional options for a faculty. For example, instructional assistants can supervise students working independently, in learning teams, in testing centers, or in apprenticeship projects. Clerical aides or volunteers can distribute and maintain an accountability system for materials. General aides can supervise students at lunch, before and after school, set up labs and move equipment. A technician can maintain computers and teach students and teachers how to use various equipment. Student teachers can serve as quasiprofessionals making presentations, writing materials, and conducting seminars.

Resource centers for specific disciplines, a combination of disciplines, or topic study are supervised by teachers and instructional assistants. Students report to the resource centers to work on units and contracts and projects. While in the resource centers, students work alone, in pairs or with a learning team. At least one teacher is available to provide help to the students as needed. The number of students in a resource area at any one time depends on space availability. Presentations, depending on their nature, can be offered to large groups of students in an auditorium or similar spaces. The idea of presenting a film, a video or a lecture four or five times per day to different groups of students seems a poor use of teacher time. Assuming the availability of suitable space and equipment, presentations can be given once to all the students who need to experience it, thus freeing teachers to use the time saved to do other things. When teachers are not restricted by five classes per day with 30 students each, they are able to do research, advise and coach students, develop curriculum, and plan instruction.

Students assigned to community work can be supervised by volunteer mentors who receive guidance from a coordinator of outreach. The outreach coordinator can be assigned to a teacher as a partial or collateral responsibility. The outreach coordinator job maintains communication with mentors in community placements, arranges for student transportation as needed, and monitors the work of both students and mentors.

Keeping track of student progress requires the cooperation of several persons. Computers in each resource center networked to teacher adviser workstations and the guidance center can monitor and record student progress. As students complete units, contracts, and other work associated with academic progress, notice of completion can be placed in a database to be accessed as needed. Clerical assistants enter the data into the databases. Electronic transfer of records among schools in a district and state have reduced the time required to communicate information about students leaving the school. Similar arrangements are possible with institutions of higher learning, the military, and some employers. It seems only a matter of time before the idea of report cards will be replaced by an electronic system that gives parents and guardians instant access to student progress.

The school as a learning environment is guided by administrators, teachers, paraprofessionals, nonprofessional staff, volunteers, and student teachers. Each division within a school is a microcosm of the larger one. Each teacher adviser manages a learning environment for his or her advisees. Each teacher as coach creates a learning environment for his or her students. And, in essence, each student designs a learning environment for his or her personal learning. The focus of the totality is to provide for students, regardless of talents, interests, and background, a program of learning that is good for them and in which they may succeed.

ACTION STEPS

+ Arrange a visit to the Thomas Haney Secondary Centre in Maple Ridge, British Columbia, or read "A High School for All Reasons," *International Journal of Educational Reform*, April, 1993, to learn about the mechanics of a student-driven schedule.

+ Investigate different approaches to block scheduling. List the assumptions underlying each. What are their advantages and disadvantages?

+ Create a plan for moving a high school from a traditional schedule to a block schedule to a student-driven schedule. Establish a time line and procedures for achieving this end.

8

MOTIVATION AND LEARNING

Watching children report to kindergarten on the first day of school is instructive. They arrive with a great deal of excitement and anticipation. It is a indeed a special day in their lives; it is a day for which they have waited a long time. Certainly there is some trepidation and even a few tears, but the overwhelming effect is positive. The children see school as a place to add quality to their lives. Nine years later the same children arrive at the high school. Some come with the same enthusiasm and motivation to learn. But for many, school isn't fun anymore.

If the negative effect from schooling was only associated with a minority of students, the problem would be much less. A general belief exists among secondary educators, for example, that the ninth grade is a major problem area. Many students fail; more are turned off by the school curriculum, the teachers, and the school itself. School districts and schools establish special task forces to address the problems of grade nine. Obviously something happens from grade one through grade nine that changes student perception of school as a valued place where one's needs are consistently met. What are the causes of this phenomenon? Why do so many students fail to see school as a value? To answer these questions, it is helpful to examine the basic issues of human needs.

BASIC NEEDS

The psychiatrist William Glasser (1986) asserts that all human behavior is aimed at meeting five basic needs: survival, belonging, power, freedom, and fun. People are internally motivated throughout their lives to satisfy these needs. Glasser acknowledges that differences exist among people in the strength of the needs, but all human beings live their lives in ways that will best satisfy one or more of these needs at any given time. Sometimes the needs can be conflicting, as when a person works hard to gain a promotion at work (power), but does so at the expense of quality time with the family (belonging).

According to Glasser, when needs are met, people feel pleasure. When needs are not met, people feel pain. Significant people, places, events, and experiences are those that contribute to the satisfaction of one's basic needs. Over time, people store these "need satisfiers" in their memories. When they are no longer perceived as need satisfiers, they are gradually removed from a position of significance.

For the kindergarten child, school is perceived as a need satisfier. It is part of the child's quality world. When school experiences enable students to meet one or more of their basic needs, school remains in the student's quality world. When it does not, it is slowly removed. Once removed, it is difficult to restore. High school educators, in particular, face this kind of problem.

Abraham Maslow (1970) believed that individuals seek to satisfy a hierarchy of needs on five levels. Physiological needs are the lowest; safety needs are next. The third level is the need for belonging and love. Esteem needs (achievement, recognition, status, appreciation) constitute the fourth level. The highest level of the hierarchy is the need for self-actualization. Maslow placed these needs on a pyramid to illustrate that the higher needs are more important than the lower ones. As needs at the bottom of the pyramid are satisfied, the higher needs are free to emerge. People who are unable to satisfy lower needs rarely get to levels three, four or five.

Similarities can readily be seen between the basic needs as proposed by Glasser and those proposed by Maslow. The survival needs of Glasser resemble the physiological and safety needs of Maslow. The need for belonging or love is a match. Glasser's need for power correlates with Maslow's esteem needs and even the need for self-actualization (realizing one's full talent and potential). Only the needs for fun and freedom appear to differ. The need for freedom, of course, may be one of the preconditions for satisfying the basic needs in Maslow's hierarchy. Glasser feels strongly that fun is a natural accompaniment to learning something new and valuable.

The main difference between the theories resides in the concept of hierarchy. Maslow's representation assumes that some needs are more important than others; Glasser disagrees. In his view, the most important need is the one that presently is not satisfied. The importance of any of the five needs is relative to the individual and the circumstances in which he or she finds himself or herself. The two theories, however, are similar and provide a useful basis for a discussion of motivation and learning.

THE ART OF PERSUASION

Motivation is important because it contributes significantly to student achievement. Students who are motivated generally do well in school. Correspondingly, students who are not motivated generally do not do as well in school. Motivation, however, is not synonymous with achievement, nor can it be inferred by looking at the results of standardized tests (Ames, 1990). Student achievement is determined by a number of factors. In some cases, achievement is immediate and short-term; in other cases, the motivation to achieve is an outcome of learning and flows from a goal and commitment to lifelong learning. As Ames (1990) observed, "We not only want students to achieve, we want them to value the process of learning and the improvement of their skills, we want them to willingly put forth the necessary effort to develop and apply their skills and knowledge, and we want them to develop a long-term commitment to learning" (p. 410).

Motivation theory is dominated by two distinct approaches. The first, based on Thorndike's Law of Effect formulated in 1898, argues that behavior leading to a positive consequence will likely be repeated. Later, B.F. Skinner described the rewards that followed behaviors as reinforcements, which increased the likelihood that the behavior(s) would recur. He asserted that if we want people to behave in a certain way, we must get them to behave that way and then reinforce the behavior with a reward valuable to the individual.

The second approach to motivation defines learning as individual and self-regulated. Students choose to learn or not to learn. All external stimuli are filtered through the internal world of the learner. Since everyone's experiences are idiosyncratic, responding to stimuli is a matter of individual choice. The familiar formula, "Do this, and you will get that," works only when the that is worth getting and the this is worth doing. Humans can reflect on an external stimulus, judge its value, and choose to respond in a way that may or may not be consistent with what the person offering the reward had in mind.

EXTRINSIC REWARDS

Rewarding people for doing what we want them to do is familiar to all of us. In fact, the process is so deeply ingrained in the human psyche that it seems like common sense. Because the process appears so sensible, it is practiced as a regular part of human interaction. Parents promise their children toys, candy, trips, and other rewards for being good. Some even offer money for good grades in school, a kind of reward for a reward. Most, if not all schools, operate on the belief that extrinsic rewards are effective in motivating students to learn what they are supposed to learn. For example, those who learn the most are rewarded with the highest grades. Honor rolls are created to offer an additional reward to high achieving students. Rank-in-class figures in deciding who will be acknowledged as valedictorian, salutatorian, or in the top 10 in the graduating class. These rewards are deemed appropriate for students who have achieved and appropriate stimuli to achievement for other students.

The opposite end of the reward continuum is punishment. Students who fail to achieve are graded accordingly. Like higher grades, failure is expected to spur students to higher achievement; avoidance of failure is reason to buckle down in school and do the required work. Rewards reinforce appropriate behavior, while failure extinguishes inappropriate behavior. Grades, trophies, gold stars, stickers are all offered as incentives for students to do the schoolwork. If indeed these motivators worked universally, chances are there would be little or no school failure. All students would respond with equal intensity for learning. They would choose to do willingly what schools require.

Skinner felt that praise was "the greatest tool in behavior modification." He recommended that parents and teachers catch children doing something right and praise them for it. Teachers are frequently exhorted to praise students for good performances. Although praise may indeed cause students to value a behavior or perceive themselves more positively, indiscriminate praise can lead students to value the praise at the expense of the learning. Rowe (1974) found that students whose teachers frequently used praise showed less task persistence than their peers and were less likely to share ideas with their fellow students.

Extrinsic rewards are overused in schools. When students get to the high school years they often expect rewards for doing work. They respond best to extrinsic control, and in so doing, lose sight of the reason for their learning. When the reward becomes more important than the learning, students lose sense of the value of schooling. Used properly, extrinsic incentives can be effective in getting students to transfer the good feelings that come with a reward to the task itself. This is especially effective, according to Brophy (1987), when the learning task involves practice designed to produce mastery of specific skills. Brophy sees extrinsic incentives as more effective for stimulating *intensity of effort* than for inducing thoughtfulness or quality of performance. For example, to help students take more responsibility for correcting inappropriate behavior, getting them to please the teacher or the adult can be an initial step in reversing negative behavior. In time, however, it would be necessary to remove the external incentive so that the students could behave more responsibly on their own.

Other researchers (Boggiano, et al., 1987; Jackson, 1968) warn against the indiscriminate use of external rewards with groups of students because this overlooks individual differences. Lepper and Cordova (1992) discovered that when promised a reward for doing well on a problem-solving task, students were less systematic in their approach and took longer than students for whom no reward was offered. Apparently emphasis on the reward caused the students to focus less on the task itself and more on getting the task completed.

INTRINSIC MOTIVATION

Rewards can also be inherent to the task itself. Students who are intrinsically motivated participate in learning activities for their own sake as compared to the extrinsically motivated who participate to receive a reward or avoid a punishment. In line with Glasser and Maslow, intrinsic motivation appears related to the need for achievement, recognition, or power. Its essence is the emergence of *interest* as students respond to challenges in the environment. The measure of a person's skills against the challenge is personal feedback from the experience. Feedback tells the person how closely he or she is able to do what he or she wants to do. Skills increase and strengthen in challenges (Czikszentmihalyi, 1978). It is important that challenges are neither too easy nor too difficult. Students not only react well to moderate challenges, they tend to seek them out. Danner and Lonkey (1981) have shown "that children appeared to be intrinsically motivated to engage in those tasks which were within their reach but developmentally just beyond their current level" (p. 1046).

In his popular book, *Flow*, Czikszentmihalyi (1990) describes the motivation that individuals display who undertake such arduous activities as mountain climbing or marathon running. Each activity exemplifies a *challenge* the individual chooses to undertake. The commitment of time and effort naturally flows from an internal desire to achieve personal goals associated with the activity. The relationship of goal to competency is dynamic. As the individual's skill level increases, the expectancy level correspondingly increases. The individual essentially assigns his or her own homework.

Many school situations exemplify intrinsic motivation at work—the activities where students are happily concentrated. Students are not simply busy completing worksheets or other less challenging tasks; they are engaged in serious study. Varsity athletes are willing to devote more hours to practice than they usually do to academic study. They are willing to endure an excess of hardships in order to improve their skills and enhance the likelihood participating in interscholastic competitions. Music students know the necessity of rehearsals and daily practice. The computer aficionado misses lunch to debug a program or create an electronic bulletin board or surf the Internet. Science students commit endless hours to collecting their data and reporting their findings. In all these experiences, the appeal is in the *task*. The external rewards, if any, are perceived as secondary. For most of these students, the rewards lie in the good feelings that accompany the act of learning something new.

COMPARING EXTRINSIC AND INTRINSIC REWARDS

In a school setting, both extrinsic and intrinsic rewards serve to motivate students to learn. The real issue is: when is one more appropriate than the other. Deci's (1978) summary of research findings, although somewhat dated, may prove helpful:

1. Extrinsic rewards that are salient and contingent upon performing an activity tend to decrease people's intrinsic motivation for doing interesting activities.

2. When extrinsic rewards are used so that they primarily convey information that a person is competent and self-determining and they aren't intended as controllers of behavior, they tend to enhance rather than undermine intrinsic motivation.

3. Extrinsic rewards tend to impair people's performance on open-ended activities such as problem-solving.

4. Extrinsic rewards tend to improve performance on routine, well-learned activities (p. 197).

More recently, Lepper (1988) found that extrinsically oriented students tend to gravitate toward tasks that are relatively easy and appear to be more interested in putting forth the least amount of effort for the maximum benefit. The specific goals of a learning task are important factors in choosing one kind of reward system over another. Short-term learning may need extrinsic motivators; long-term learning seems more aligned with an intrinsic orientation. As the goals of education begin to place more emphasis upon problem solving and lifelong learning, educators will need to seek better ways to build on individual students' intrinsic motivation. All humans are internally motivated to satisfy basic needs. The key to learning and motivation seems to be a matter of convincing students that it is in their best interests to learn what the school suggests. The will to learn must precede the what to learn.

CREATING MOTIVATIONAL SCHOOL ENVIRONMENTS

What happens to students in the school setting can have a major impact on their motivation to learn. Students bring different motivational histories to the school. If all were highly motivated to take advantage of schooling, there would be few problems. At the college and university level all students choose to be there. Unfortunately, this is not so at the K-12 level. This condition makes precollegiate teaching a very difficult profession. Schools must be prepared to accept students wherever they are and advance them accordingly. What specifically can building level educators do to facilitate student motivation and learning?

THE TOTAL SCHOOL

General school policy must support the idea that all students can and will learn. When this idea is written in policy, it implies that teachers and administrators are responsible for finding ways to enable all students to achieve success. A school without failure is not one where students do not make mistakes or where grades are given regardless of attainment or effort, but rather an environment where students see themselves as capable and competent. School personnel take special care to encourage student efforts to learn. No student feels embarrassed or fears criticism for making mistakes. Mistakes are seen as part of the learning process. Each student is part of a community of learners.

CLASSROOM MEETINGS

Classroom meetings—where students have an opportunity to respond to open-ended questions in a nonthreatening atmosphere—can be scheduled as a regular part of a student's experiences. These meetings can focus on topics of interest to students, or student problems, or serve as feedback about the efficacy of instruction. Glasser (1969) and Jenkins (1996) offer practical suggestions for conducting such meetings. Socratic seminars (Adler, 1982) can also be scheduled on a regular basis in which students discuss the meaning of great ideas in such documents as the *Declaration of Independence*, *The Preamble to the Constitution*, and Lincoln's *Gettysburg Address*. The sources are infinite and can be arranged so that different themes are addressed at different times during the school year. Bennett's *The Book of Virtues* (1993) is an excellent reference for launching Socratic seminars in a school setting.

CURRICULUM

It is the responsibility of the teaching faculty to help students see the connection between the curriculum and the real world. Teachers must explain to students why specific content is worth learning, either in its own right or as a step to more challenging learning. Brophy (1987) captures the relationship between curriculum and motivation in the following statement, "It is not reasonable to expect students to be motivated to learn if they are continually expected to practice skills already thoroughly mastered, memorize lists for no good reason, copy definitions of terms that are never used, or read material that is not meaningful to them because it is too vague, abstract, or foreign to their experience" (p. 42).

Much of what students are asked to learn in school has no relevance to improving the quality of their lives, either present or future. Textbook teaching still dominates as teachers cover the chapters sequentially. Curriculum that is focused on concepts, themes, and problems, and that uses multiple resources has a greater likelihood of stimulating student interest. Staffing patterns organized around teacher strengths can benefit more students than the single teacher in the traditional self-contained classroom. Flexible scheduling can adjust time to the learning task, thus capitalizing on student interest.

INSTRUCTION

The way to help students succeed in the long run is to have them succeed in the short run and consistently. Nothing seems to be more motivational than consistent improvement at tasks which students perceive as meaningful. The notion of high expectations succeeds only when students can achieve them with reasonable effort. Instruction focused on individual students should begin with the knowledge and skill levels they bring to the learning act and proceed accordingly. When students perceive themselves as able to do the work, they are more likely to expend the necessary effort to succeed.

LEARNING STYLE

Diagnosing and accommodating individual student learning style contributes to motivation for learning. An abundance of research supports the value of retraining weak cognitive skills and matching instruction with student style preferences. In general, the findings reveal that students' achievement increases, their attitude toward school becomes more positive, and behavioral difficulties decrease. For example, hands-on learning can be highly motivational for students who display a preference for learning with manipulatives. Short assignments can help students with low persistence achieve and gain momentum for continued achievement. Students are interested in knowing their learning style and its implication for how to structure their learning and study time.

ADVISEMENT

The implementation of an advisement program for all students promotes a sense of community throughout the school. When each professional member of the school staff serves as an adviser, a manageable ratio of advisers to advisees is possible. Advisers get to know their advisees well enough to offer appropriate advice to them and to provide salient information about them to other teachers. The adviser helps to develop an educational plan for each advisee. These plans, similar to the IEP's of exceptional students, identify appropriate goals and coursework to help individual students succeed in school. Research on achievement motivation (Dweck & Elliott, 1983) has shown that effort and persistence are greater when students set reasonable goals.

COOPERATIVE LEARNING

Cooperative learning is the name given to various instructional methods in which students from all levels of achievement work together in small groups toward a common goal. Several researchers (Johnson & Johnson, 1986; Slavin, 1993) have found that, compared with traditional instruction, cooperative learning results in higher motivation for more students to achieve and more positive attitudes toward both teachers and subject matter. There are several approaches to cooperative learning, but common elements include face-to-face interaction among students, positive interdependence, and equal opportunity for success.

Cooperative learning can be applied to any subject area. Different methods, however, may be more suitable for some areas than others. Since the goal is to have all students learn and to share positive experiences, careful planning of both content and group composition is necessary. Johnson and Johnson estimate that typically only 7–20% of student time is spent working in cooperative learning activities. They recommend 60–70%.

Teaching students how to function effectively in collaborative groups seems a necessity. Working cooperatively with other like-minded individuals is almost always highly motivating. Cooperative groups enable students to work together toward common ends and in the process develop a healthy respect for each other. As technology expands learning possibilities, students may even conduct academic inquiries with students in other geographic areas.

CHOICES

Few people respond favorably to mandates. When students are offered options in curriculum and instructional activities, it appeals to their basic need for freedom or autonomy.

Developing alternative pathways to common ends is one way of providing choices for students. Typically, schools give students little or no choice in meeting learning objectives. Courses can be organized as units or projects so that students may progress at their own rate. Flexible scheduling can offer students opportunities to devote more or less time to learning tasks. Options can be provided through a well-planned program of independent study where students work in a specific area under the tutelage of faculty and community mentors. Options should be available to all.

MOTIVATION AND RELUCTANT LEARNERS

Some students need more assistance than others. These at-risk students have usually experienced a history of failure in school and see no reason to work hard. They attend school until they are old enough to dropout or take the GED. Their motivation to learn what school has to offer seems nonexistent. In many respects they harbor so much animosity toward typical schools and teachers that they need a complete change in learning environment—a new venue. Special venues are usually characterized by small student-teacher ratios, a caring team of professionals, opportunities to earn credit toward graduation, much one-on-one help, interesting curriculum, and flexible scheduling. Many at-risk students have few or no credits toward graduation. It is not surprising that their motivation to continue with formal schooling has almost disappeared since their transcripts mostly report failures. Initially at-risk students must be helped to see themselves as learners. For many of these youngsters, ineffective cognitive processing skills contribute to their lack of school success. Diagnosing students' skills of analysis, discrimination, categorization, and memory is a beginning point. Training programs can then be established to strengthen these general learning skills. Such programs can progress from the general to the specific so that students can ultimately learn how to transfer the skills to various academic and problem solving settings.

Reluctant learners often have not learned how to learn. Consequently, they have had little or no success in school. Many reluctant learners attribute what success they have had in school to luck and not to effort. In essence, they have not developed what some educators call a "can do" attitude. Their "locus of control" for success is external, not internal. They must be helped to change if they are to become self-sufficient learners. Such efforts may require considerably more resources than are needed for regular programs, but these students are more truly in need.

Using nonacademic experiences is a stepping stone to help reluctant students gain a sense of power in academic settings. For example, outward bound experiences enable students to use their physical ability to solve problems and to accomplish challenging tasks. A program for at-risk learners developed at George Mason University, Fairfax, Virginia, includes exercises that teach students to break boards with their hands as a motivator. A middle school in Miami, Florida, teaches students how to juggle to increase motivation for learning. The point in all three cases is to break through mental barriers and build on successes with tasks students basically believe they could not do.

Brophy's recommendations for attribution retraining are helpful in developing guidelines for reluctant learners: (1) Help students to concentrate on tasks rather than become distracted by fear of failure; (2) Help students reflect on errors and figure out alternative ways to approach a problem rather than give up; and (3) Help students see that mistakes are the result of insufficient effort, lack of information, or reliance on ineffective strategies rather than low ability (Brophy, 1986). These three recommendations imply a different philosophy about teaching and learning. Applied to a total school program, they would likely improve learning motivation for all students. Reluctant learners, however, are a special case. They frequently irritate principals and teachers who in turn irritate them. The resolution to this dilemma is not to remove them from the school, but rather to provide a program that builds efficacy one step at a time. Too often, remedial programs simply reduce class size while maintaining a traditional instructional program. A school-within-a-school or cognitive apprenticeship with ample flexibility may offer greater hope for student success.

MOTIVATION IN PERSPECTIVE

According to Glasser (1969), secondary schools are not and have not been concerned with the psychological needs of students, especially the need for power. Most schools are survival oriented. Students may meet their psychological needs at home or in extracurricular activities, but they are not likely to do so in schoolwork. For many students, the middle school years terminate their serious involvement with formal education. School does not occupy a significant place in their quality worlds.

Motivation to learn can be conceptualized as a general trait or a situation-specific state (Brophy, 1987). As a general trait, it is characterized by a desire to learn no matter what the subject matter or topic. People just want to do well regardless of the task. As a situation-specific trait, it refers to a desire to do well at a particular task or in a particular subject field. In some cases, motivation for a specific subject may transfer from a well-liked teacher to the subject matter itself. The role of the teacher in generating enthusiasm for learning can not be overstated. When teachers become significant people in the eyes of students, they help generate student interest in learning tasks.

Most children begin school with enthusiasm for learning. School is firmly fixed in their positive system of values. Over time, however, the importance begins to diminish as school experiences fail to connect with their lives. Corey (1944), in his essay "The Poor Scholar's Soliloquy," captures the plight of many students in this poignant account of a boy who doesn't fit the curriculum he must follow but who will succeed in spite of it. He writes:

> I don't do very well in arithmetic either. Seems I can't keep my mind on the problems. We had one the other day like this:
>
>> If a 57 foot telephone pole falls across a cement highway so that 17 3/6 feet extend from one side and 14 9/17 feet the other, how wide is the highway?
>
> That seemed to me like an awfully silly way to get the width of a highway. I didn't even try to answer it

because it didn't say whether the pole had fallen straight across or not. . . . Dad says I can quit school when I'm fifteen and I'm sort of anxious to because there are a lot of things I want to learn how to do and as my uncle says, I'm not getting any younger (p. 220).

Mary Leonhardt, in her insightful book, *Parents Who Love Reading, Kids Who Don't* (1993), wonders why school libraries and media centers don't stock a healthy supply of popular books and comics to get students interested in using the facility. She writes, "In a bid for a child's attention, a Batman comic might have a chance over a rock video—but a beautifully illustrated book on how the Hopi Indians planted corn probably isn't even in the running" (p. 27).

Most students who turn off to the ways of formal schooling suffer in varying degrees from not knowing how to learn. Research in cognitive psychology has identified several cognitive processing skills needed for successful learning. If students are weak in specific skills, they have little chance of succeeding at a moderate or high level in learning tasks that require their use, even in a supportive learning environment. For example, if a prerequisite for completing an assignment is analysis, students who are strong analyzers will likely do well, but those who are not will simply be frustrated. Their performance or lack of it has nothing to do with innate ability. Schools must help all learners improve their skills as learners, but especially those with a history of school failure.

The principal as instructional leader is the key to building a school learning community. Students must feel they belong to the school in order to participate fully. Their participation is contingent upon their acceptance as persons and their ability to succeed with the curriculum. The selection and deployment of staff are both critical decisions of the school principal. Selecting teachers who see their roles as more than dispensers of subject matter can help create a supportive learning environment.

Schools and teachers today are under incredible pressure from policymakers to do more for students. The principal must help others understand the findings of Deci, et al. (1982): "When teachers are themselves pressured toward particular outcomes, they may in turn become more controlling with their students, which could decrease the intrinsic motivation and self esteem of those students" (p. 853). Intrinsic motivation is the stuff from which a desire for lifelong learning germinates. Schools must make it a high priority.

ACTION STEPS

♦ Arrange to visit the Key School (K-5) or the Key Renaissance School in Indianapolis, Indiana. Both schools apply the theory of multiple intelligences proposed by Howard Gardner of Harvard University. Learning experiences for students in each of the seven intelligences are planned each day. In addition, at the Key School students are scheduled three times per week into an area called "Flow" where they are free to choose among a variety of academic games. Teachers observe the students to discover where they are "happily concentrated."

♦ Read *Flow: The Psychology of Optimal Experience* (1990) by Mihaly Czikszentmihalyi. List the implications his ideas have for school programs.

♦ Examine some of the current programs, such as "Book-It," designed to get students to read more. What assumptions support these programs? What are the advantages and disadvantages? Redesign one of the programs to tap intrinsic motivation.

♦ Investigate either the classroom meeting (Educator Training Center, 117 East 8th Street, Suite 810, Long Beach, CA 90813) or the Socratic seminar (*The Paideia Proposals* (1982), Mortimer Adler). Develop a plan to implement one of them in a school setting.

9

ACTION RESEARCH

Reform has been a part of the school vernacular for years. Each decade seems to bring a new idea for improving schools. In the 1950s, the comprehensive model was seen as the salvation of the high school. The 1960s brought a plethora of reform efforts from ungraded, multiage classrooms to team teaching. Back to basics dominated the 1970s as states instituted basic skills testing to guarantee minimal performance for all high school graduates. The report, *A Nation at Risk*, captured the attention of educators in the 1980s as schools moved to increase graduation requirements, lengthen the school day, and raise expectations. Effective schools were viewed as orderly, humane institutions with high expectations for all students and frequent monitoring of student progress.

Most of these reform efforts failed to effect any lasting change at the school level. Apparently reform was easier to postulate than accomplish. Educators wrote and talked about reform, but change required that they do something, and doing is always more arduous than talking. Indeed, many of the reform efforts originated in state legislatures, state departments of education and universities. Local educators complained about micro-management of schools by persons who were not familiar with local school conditions.

The school as the locus of change became the clarion call of the 1990s. School-based councils composed of parents, teachers, administrators, community leaders, and students gathered together to plan for individual school improvement. School improvement plans were written to provide short and long range guidance. Individual schools, school districts, state educational agencies, and state legislatures hoped to work together for school improvement. Unfortunately, the tension between state control and local control continued in various forms. One message was clear, however; local decision-making for school improvement will continue in one form or another as schools prepare for the 21st century and beyond.

Local decision-making can take several forms. It can be seen in school-based councils which meet regularly to discuss school progress. It can be seen in school renewal projects which are gradually replacing the familiar 5- and 10-year school accreditations. It can be seen in the practice of giving teachers a voice in the formulation of school budgets. It can be seen in the practice of individual educators and groups of educators asking questions about pedagogy and gathering data to determine what approaches are effective and for whom. It is to this latter practice that this final chapter is addressed.

HISTORICAL PERSPECTIVE

In 1953, Stephen M. Corey, then the Director of the Horace Mann Lincoln Institute of School Experimentation, Teachers College, Columbia University, wrote *Action Research to Improve School Practices*. It was Corey's belief that the chasm between educational research and educational practice could be reduced when classroom teachers engaged in a form of classroom research aimed at improving their instructional decision-making. He labeled the practice "action research" to differentiate it from more formal research usually found in universities. The idea that classroom teachers could engage in hands-on research was an adaptation of the work of Kurt Lewin who used research as an intervention strategy for solving social problems. According to Lewin, action research "consisted of analysis, fact-finding, conceptualization, planning, execution, more fact-finding or evaluation, and then a repetition of the whole circle of activities, indeed a spiral of such circles" (Lewin, 1948).

Action research, sometimes called practitioner or teacher research, places the control of school improvement in the hands of teachers, groups of teachers, and building-level administrators. It acknowledges that theory and practice go hand-in-hand, and that practitioners are capable of reflecting critically upon what they do with the aim of improving it. Teachers actually do the research in their classrooms, or instructional areas, rather than read about it.

The term action research implies that some action will be taken and analyzed to determine its effectiveness. Action research begins with the questions that educators have about the practice of teaching. The process differs from more formal research in its relevance to the lives of educators and in the degree of generalizability of the findings. Corey warned that action research had many limitations. He was not even certain the results derived from one group of students could be generalized by the same teacher to his or her students in succeeding years. Compared with less systematic efforts, however, it is a decided improvement. Engaging in the process itself, moreover, tends to raise the professional level of the educator.

WHAT IS ACTION RESEARCH?

All research involves systematically accumulating and interpreting evidence, but action research focuses on evidence that helps school practitioners to determine whether their actions help students reach desirable ends. Corey (1953) identified two main aspects that appear to be as valid today as they were over 40 years ago: (1) a desirable goal and (2) a proposed action for achieving the goal . In fact, the act of teaching could be described by the same two aspects. A lesson plan, unit of work, or learning guide is literally a proposal for producing desired results in student learning. Unfortunately these tools are usually not utilized in this manner. Typically, they are repeated, discarded, or modified based largely on the intuitive judgment of teachers rather than upon substantial evidence.

The process of action research informs educators in a variety of ways, but most importantly, it helps answer questions about teaching and learning. The answers are used to improve the teaching process. Sometimes more questions are raised during the process than are answered, which deepens the inquiry and starts the process anew.

The quest for school improvement so prevalent today seems a natural setting for a resurgence of the notion that educators individually and collectively can raise the level of learning in the schools of the nation. Traditionally, building-level educators have not inquired deeply into the nature of instruction. They have been content to take direction from outside sources. The current window of opportunity can enable educators to take effective control of their professional lives. By asking questions about teaching and learning and engaging in a systematic process for answering them, educators can establish a school culture supportive of innovation and more effective learning.

ASSUMPTIONS

Several key assumptions serve as the basis for conducting action research at the school level:

- Translating theory into practice is best achieved when practitioners are involved in collecting the data from which theory is derived. (Corey used to remind his students, "If it doesn't work, it isn't good theory.")
- Local decision-making liberates educators from the mandates of external control and places trust in their professional judgment.
- Educators' questions about instruction are the best bases for research to improve school practice.
- Educators can learn to do action research in school settings.
- The process of action research is as important as the product.
- The more that recommendations for school improvement are derived from the setting in which they are to be implemented, the higher the degree of commitment on the part of the professional staff.

To engage in action research, educators need to know how to do it. Several teacher education programs offer preservice experiences in action research (Jenkins, 1994; Flake, Kuhs, Donnelly, & Ebert, 1995), but few experienced educators are equipped to apply the approach in local schools. In fact, until recently, British and Canadian educators were more inclined to use action research methods than Americans.

TYPES OF ACTION RESEARCH

Action research usually comes in two forms—quantitative and qualitative. Both have their place in school improvement and both are valuable. Quantitative action research collects data so that the relationship of one set of facts to another can be studied. Scientific techniques are used to produce quantified, and where possible, generalizable conclusions. Qualitative action researchers are more concerned with individuals' perceptions of the world. They seek personal insights rather than statistical analyses.

Quantitative and qualitative action research are alike in that they must be rigorously conducted, ongoing, and continuous. Which approach to use depends on the nature of the inquiry and the skills of the investigator(s). As educators attempt action research, they increase their awareness of improved instructional practice. They begin to internalize the belief that instructional decisions based on carefully collected evidence are better than testimony, blind faith, and tradition. The process appears similar to what the Japanese label *kaizen*—gradual, ongoing, and continuous improvement. Effective action researchers continually review, evaluate, and improve their practices.

One difference between the quantitative and qualitative approaches, however, is found in the amount of flexibility permitted by each. Quantitative action research usually proceeds straightforwardly from a hypothesis and design that rarely change during the inquiry process. The hypothesis, action statement, and design of the project establish a blueprint for conducting the study. Qualitative action research is more flexible in that questions and anticipated outcomes are often revised throughout the project. Even unanticipated outcomes are encouraged. In some cases, the two approaches feed off each other. It is common for some quantitative techniques to be used in qualitative studies and vice versa.

The decision to engage in action research arises from the desire to improve schools, and specifically instruction. Educators are engulfed by articles, books, consultants, staff development programs, and university coursework that provide information about any number of promising practices to improve teaching and learning. Unfortunately, much of this information is the work of publishing companies with products to sell or "experts" who wish to advance their pet theories. In many cases, the research base is sketchy or nonexistent.

THE PROCESS

Action research begins with a genuine desire to improve a situation; it emanates from perceiving a disparity between legitimate aspirations and the status quo. A teacher may be dissatisfied with the level of academic progress a group of students is experiencing. The teacher may be concerned about the types of questions asked by students and whether or not they lead to higher order thinking. The process is initiated by a careful assessment of the status quo and an examination of the feasible alternatives, followed by diagnosis of the reasons for the disparity. The status quo assessment must be relevant, accurate, penetrating, and as extensive as time and the skills of the teacher(s) make possible. The diagnosis must be confirmed by evidence, or it will provide a misleading basis for possible actions.

Next, a search is conducted for promising actions to reduce or eliminate the influence of forces maintaining the status quo disparity. Ideas for actions can spring from many different sources—articles, research studies, brainstorming sessions, or theories. The teacher(s) identifies the problem, chooses an action and designs an implementation strategy.

The action is then carried out. Data are collected; assessments are made; and generalizations considered. In action research, the interest is not so much in generalizing findings to a larger population, but rather in changing the behavior of the teacher or changing the practices in a given instructional area.

The process is conducted by teachers and other educators working alone, in pairs or in teams. The process can be part of a larger whole designed to examine the impact of an innovative practice on the total school. Hopkins (1993) observed that the difference between classroom research of the 1970s and the 1990s is that today it is conducted within a whole school context as opposed to within the boundaries of a particular classroom. There are many avenues to school improvement. An appropriate one might involve an entire professional team gathering data to determine the relative effectiveness of a specific innovation. Educators interested in examining the impact of cooperative learning on student achievement and student attitudes, for example, could meet regularly to plan implementation strategies, share successes, provide mutual help, and make recommendations for the school as a whole.

PREPARING EDUCATORS TO CONDUCT ACTION RESEARCH PROJECTS

Since the emphasis of action research is the improvement of instruction through an understanding of the dynamics of one's own teaching, it makes sense to involve teachers and administrators with a hands-on approach to learning the process. Motivation for learning the process, however, must precede any attempt at sharpening individual skills. A presentation by a valued staff member or an outside expert may be a good starting point. Incorporating reflective practice into the school improvement process may be the next step. For example, school improvement councils could request special action research projects as part of a school improvement plan.

Teachers can learn to develop case studies about problem students or interview selected students to determine their understanding of key concepts. (Teachers can practice their interviewing skills and their ability to create safe environments by interviewing one another.) The case study approach enables the would-be teacher-researcher to examine one student in depth and to propose various alternatives for working with the student. The student's cognitive-learning style, learning history, and experiential background in school and a specific subject are important ingredients for an in-depth case study. All relevant available information about a given student must be collected. This information serves as the basis for a learning plan for the student. The results of the plan's implementation provide feedback to determine its success. The individual case study enables the teacher-researcher to become more informed about the appropriateness of different instructional approaches for individual students. As one novice teacher-researcher observed, "After conducting a systematic case study on a student, I was never able to think of teaching all students the same way again."

Another useful activity for the beginning researcher is to examine test scores for individual students on file in the guidance area. What information is available? How can it be interpreted? Teachers must learn to look at the results of all tests *differently*. When students answer a multiple choice question incorrectly, did they answer another question correctly by choosing that answer? Instead of simply marking questions right or wrong, teachers should carefully analyze students' responses to inform future instruction. The emphasis here is upon using existing classroom activities in different ways.

These starter activities serve as training for more complex inquiries. At the next stage, teachers, working in pairs or in researcher teams, generate a list of questions which they would like to answer about their daily instruction. From this list, one or two priorities are chosen. Data are collected to determine the extent of the problem(s) and to speculate on causation. The questions are then rephrased as hypotheses or focus questions to guide the inquiry. After the questions have been rephrased, anticipated outcomes of the study can be generated. The purpose of anticipating outcomes is to guide the selection of data gathering instruments.

A review of the literature is conducted next to determine if similar inquiries have been made and to familiarize the teacher-researchers with the topic. The review may also suggest the design of the study and possible data collection instruments that can be used or modified for the study.

The research design is guided by the original question(s). The study should provide answers to the focus question(s) and evaluate the anticipated outcomes. To accomplish this end, teachers must be familiar with the advantages and disadvantages of several data collection devices. Notetaking is critical here. See Hubbard and Power (1993) for a two-step process involving raw notes and analyzed notes. Data-gathering alternatives include surveys, questionnaires, anecdotal records, interviews, sociograms, student work samples, videotapes, audiotapes, and photographs. The nature of the study and the questions to be answered direct the selection of the instruments. In some cases standardized test results or commercially developed instruments may be useful. Several books are available to help new teacher-researchers learn about instrumentation: *Doing Your Research Project* by Judith Bell (1987), *A Teacher's Guide to Classroom Research* by David Hopkins (1987), and *The Art of Classroom Inquiry* by Ruth Hubbard and Brenda Power (1993).

Analyzing the data may require creating categories of information and indexing the observations in accord with the categories. It may also require statistical analyses of the data. Categorizing and indexing are functions more closely associated with qualitative research. Statistical analysis is usually found in quantitative action research, along with graphs, histograms and frequency distributions. Where statistical analysis is needed, knowing how to do four simple operations are basic—central tendency, variability, correlation, and chi square. None of these analyses are particularly difficult to apply. Calculators and computer programs are available to do much of the work.

During the process of data analysis, teacher-researchers may revise the question(s) or restate the original hypotheses in light of new insights. Since action research is not concerned with generalizing the results to a larger population, changes may be made throughout the process. Nonetheless, researchers must still be concerned with valid and reliable data, accurate interpretations, and sound results.

Findings and conclusions are derived from the analysis of the data. The confidence that can be placed in the findings is directly related to the quality of the analysis and the breadth of support. The more varied the sources of data that support a finding, the greater the likelihood that the finding has validity.

Action research at its best is ongoing. The answer to one question leads to several others, and the depth of new questions is inextricably related to the quality of the previous answers. As novice educator-researchers move along the developmental continuum toward mastery of the research process, their behavior becomes more professional. They achieve increasingly more control of the teaching-learning process and become generators of knowledge rather than consumers.

The journey from novice to expert is a journey of some duration. Apprenticing with a skilled colleague or working under the tutelage of a university supervisor can accelerate progress. The latter also can provide a link for collaboration between universities and schools toward school improvement. It might be feasible for a university professor to work as an on-site member of a school faculty for a time, to introduce and coordinate an action research project throughout a school.

EXAMPLES OF ACTION RESEARCH

Our first example of action research involves an attempt by two teachers of English to determine the effects of teaching *visual imagery techniques* to enhance the reading comprehension of at-risk students in a high school. The idea originated from the frustration of the teachers assigned to work with a group of 20 students who were likely to drop out of school prior to graduation. The students had strong negative attitudes about school in general and reading in particular. They had not been successful at either. They avoided reading and seemed to be just waiting until their 16th birthdays when they could legally drop out of school. Nothing the teachers did proved successful.

One of the teachers had recently read an article about the use of visual imagery and its positive impact on reading comprehension. She suggested to her colleague that maybe this classic scaffolding technique would work for their students. Both agreed that it seemed worth a try. Working with a university-based supervisor, the teachers designed an action research project to test the impact of visual imagery on reading from the students' regular history book. They asked the question, "Will the use of visual imagery improve students' reading comprehension of a history textbook?"

The teachers generated several possible outcomes from their focus question. They postulated first that students could learn to use visual imagery as a reading strategy and apply it to the reading of their history textbook. They further hypothesized that the students' overall reading comprehension would improve, and that they would learn to apply visual imagery in a variety of settings. On the negative side, they wondered if the students would be sufficiently motivated to persist with the strategies. The possible negative outcome motivated the teachers to try to help the students to value the learning strategies and to teach them creatively so that the short-term novelty effect might be extended.

A cursory review of the literature gave the researchers ideas for implementing the strategies. It also provided them with a sample research design or two that could be applied to their project. As a result, they decided to limit data collection to five students. They agreed, however, to teach the strategies to all 20 of the students.

At the start, the teachers explained to the students that they were going to be part of an experiment. The purpose of the experiment was to discover ways to make reading history more interesting, even fun. They further explained that the students would learn how to apply these new ways to other material they read in and out of school. The teachers modeled visual imagery by reading words to each other. The teacher hearing the word shared the visual image that it evoked. For example, "summer" was depicted as a beach with sun and surf. "Justice" was a balanced scale. Students paired up and practiced. This type of activity continued for several days with the teachers modeling and the students practicing. The examples became increasingly more complex.

Next, the history textbook was introduced. The teachers read passages from the text and shared the images they formed to help students understand the material. Students were asked to volunteer any images they generated that were different from the teachers. Again, this type of activity continued and gradually increased in complexity until the students were creating their own images with prompts from the teachers. Gradually the prompts were eliminated. When the students appeared to be comfortable using the strategies, ways were introduced and practiced to transfer the strategies to settings other than history.

The teachers chose to collect data using four different types of instruments. First, each maintained a *separate log*. The *log* was an account of each session with the students and their reactions (direct quotes, wherever possible). The logs allowed for independent comparisons. *Interviews* were conducted with the five targeted students using questions designed to assess student comprehension of selected material from the history book. The interviews were conducted individually and resembled an oral examination. A second interview was also held to ascertain the students' perceptions of (a) how well they were able to use visual imagery, (b) any improvement they detected in their reading of the history book and (c) whether or not they were able to transfer the skill successfully to other areas in and out of school. A written *reading comprehension test* was administered in two ways: (1) the students read a paragraph and responded by selecting the answers to several questions about the paragraph; and (2) the paragraph was available on an audiotape for students to hear and respond. They were asked to select the correct answer from several questions about the paragraph. The students' history teachers also were asked to provide a *brief progress report* on each of the five students' reading habits and their achievement in history.

From the collected data the teacher-researchers discovered that 4 of the 5 students were able to comprehend the history material more effectively. There was conflicting information from the silent and oral reading tests of the one student who did not improve. That student comprehended the material best when he could read along while listening to the audiotape of the text. The students all reported an increased interest in history and a willingness to read the history text. Their history teachers corroborated the increase in interest.

From these findings the researchers concluded that visual imagery can be taught to students effectively and that students can apply the strategies in reading a history textbook. They were unable to gather sufficient data to make any statements about transfer of visual imagery to other settings. They concluded that this was a question for a subsequent inquiry.

Overall, this project required about 100 hours of the teachers' time. The data collection instruments were thought to demand a minimum of time. The outcome, however, was well worth the time invested.

Our second example of action research focuses on the effects of learning style preference on student achievement. Two middle school teachers were involved. Both teachers had experienced a district level staff development workshop on student learning styles that emphasized the impact of matching student preferences with the physical learning environment. Specifically, the workshop presenters cited research about the relationship between an informal learning environment and school achievement. The teachers reasoned that if they were to create an informal learning environment in part of their classrooms, maybe some of the students would begin to do better.

The initial draft of their research question asked, "Does matching student preference for formal or informal posture have an effect on attitude and on-task behavior?" After reviewing some of the literature, they refined the question to read, "Does matching student preference for an informal learning environment enable the student to concentrate more effectively on learning tasks?" From the literature they concluded that changing the learning environment from formal to informal was insufficient by itself to impact student achievement significantly. They did reason, however, that if they matched students' preferences for an informal environment, the students would feel less stress and ostensibly would be better able to concentrate. To the degree that concentration contributed to effective learning, the students' learning would be affected positively. The teachers felt that the students would be able to work at tasks for longer periods of time without being distracted internally or externally.

Some form of diagnosis was required to identify the students who preferred an informal environment. The teachers opted for one of the scales of the NASSP *Learning Style Profile* (LSP) which measures students' formal vs informal posture preference. The study sample was selected from the 50 students in the combined classes. Students were placed in the sample if they scored between 14 and 16 or 4 and 6 on the posture preference scale. The higher numbers represented students who said they needed an informal setting to concentrate. The lower numbers represented students who preferred a formal setting. The result was a sample of seven informal students and 10 formal students.

The sample groups were assigned different learning environments and given several learning tasks to complete. An informal corner with carpet and comfortable furniture was created in each classroom to accommodate the informal preferences. Regular classroom desks and tables seemed sufficient for the formal preferences. Ten different learning tasks were developed. Each student in each of the groups was matched and mismatched for half of the tasks. The learning tasks were varied so as to attempt to control for the variable of student interest.

Data were collected in several ways to characterize the behavior of students in each of the settings. The first was a *check list* created by the teachers. The second was an *observation log* in which time samples were recorded. Every 5 minutes the teacher observer simply checked "on task" or "off task," depending on her assessment of the student's behavior. The results were later compared for concordance. After each of the 10 sessions, each student was asked to record in a *student log or journal* the answer to the following question, "Did the furniture in which you did your work help you pay attention to the assignment? Why or why not?" The logs were collected and compared to the teacher observations. Students were interviewed at the close of the project and asked questions about the settings and their ability to concentrate. The teachers developed a *structured interview* form to standardize the questions. *Photographs* were taken of the students working in both settings and were incorporated in the interview. Students saw themselves in both settings and were asked to discuss which one helped them concentrate better.

The researchers found that of the 17 students in the project, all seemed to work better when matched by posture preference. Both the checklists and the observation logs corroborated the impact of matching. Additionally, the students indicated that they felt more comfortable and seemed better able to concentrate in either formal or informal setting when matched. There were no reversals. When asked if they learned more, most said they weren't sure; only that they were more comfortable. An unanticipated artifact was that the informal group was all male. Eight of the 10 formal students were female.

The researchers concluded that matching students' posture preference with the physical environment can enhance their ability to concentrate on learning tasks. They saw a need to provide for informal areas in all classrooms and learning environments. The greater number of males to females preferring informal to formal led to the tentative conclusion that traditional learning environments are less friendly for male students.

In both these examples, the teacher-researchers were undertaking their first action research projects. Aside from the substantive conclusions, the teachers found themselves becoming more systematic in their approach to instruction. They felt more empowered to control their own destinies and to contribute to the success of their schools.

THE FUTURE

The American tendency for bigness leads to big projects like the New American School Development Corporation (NASDC), America 2000, national standards for subject disciplines, and international comparative testing programs. As an alternative, perhaps some school districts, in cooperation with private enterprise, could offer incentives to educators in the form of grants to conduct action research projects at the school level. A "Dewey Prize" might be given to the best piece of action research by an educator or group of educators. Research symposia at different locations could provide educators with networking opportunities and a forum to describe the nature of their inquiries. The travel and cross-pollination of ideas could raise the level of professional performance significantly.

The education of all students is best served through a constant search for better ways to teach and to learn. In practice, action research may represent a refinement of the process every teacher goes through as he or she tries to improve. A major goal of every school should be a search for more effective educational practices to enhance learning opportunities for all students. This continuous search and implementation can bring with it an ever-spiraling Hawthorne Effect where each step becomes a means rather than an end. The role of the principal and the school leadership team is to set a standard and expectation for such continuing improvement.

We would like to reiterate a point we made earlier: school restructuring does not necessarily lead to changes in instructional practice nor to improved student performance. Research on school restructuring and authentic pedagogy suggests that the connection between changes in teaching and learning behavior and changes in school structure is mediated by cultural and climate influences. School norms and expectations, teacher knowledge and skill, and stakeholder satisfaction all shape what happens in schools and classrooms.

School leaders committed to improving instruction and the environment of learning must first work to build a strong school culture that will sustain a professional community for teachers and a personalized learning environment for students. This initiative, in turn, will empower teachers to mount action research, to learn how to teach differently, and to develop the structures, like apprenticeships and advisement, that serve to create and support a vital school learning organization.

If instructional practice in our schools is to change, the building leadership team must exercise a defining role.

ACTION STEPS

   ♦ Contact a university professor with knowledge and skills in action research. Collaborate and develop a staff development plan for a cadre of teachers to conduct an action research project in a school setting.

- Obtain a copy of Stephen Corey's *Action Research to Improve School Practices* (1953). Rewrite his example of the group inquiry project to incorporate a contemporary innovative practice; e.g., cooperative groups, alternative forms of assessment, authentic pedagogy.

REFERENCES

▪A▪

Adler, M. (1982). The Paideia proposal: An educational manifesto. New York: Macmillan.

Allport, G.W., & Vernon, P.E. (1933). Studies in expressive movement. New York: Macmillan.

America 2000: An Educational Strategy. (1991). Washington, DC: US Department of Education.

Ames, C.A. (Spring, 1990). "Motivation: What teachers need to know." Teachers College Record, 91(3).

▪B▪

Baumann, J.F. (1984). "The effectiveness of a direct instruction paradigm for teaching main idea comprehension." Reading Research Quarterly, 20, 93–115.

Bell, J. (1987). Doing your research project. Philadelphia: Open University Press.

Bennet, W.J. (1993). The book of virtues. New York: Simon & Schuster.

Bennett, S.N. (1976). Teaching styles and pupil progress. London: Open Books.

Berliner, D.C. (1989). "The executive functions of teaching." In L.W. Anderson, The effective teacher: Study guide and readings. New York: Random House.

Besel, R. (July, 1973). "Diagnosis—prescription in the context of instructional management." Educational Technology.

Black, J.A., & English, F.W. (1986). What they don't tell you in schools of education about school administration. Lancaster, PA: Technomic Publishing.

Bloom, B.S., Hastings J.T., & Madaus, G.F. (1971). Handbook on formative and summative evaluation of student learning. New York: McGraw-Hill.

Boehm, R.G., & Boehm, R.D. (October, 1994). "Directions for geography students: Intellectual challenge and meaningful careers." NASSP Bulletin, 78(564), 7–18.

Boggiano, A., Barret, M., Weiher, A.W., McCleland, D.C., & Lusk, C.M. (1987). "Use of the maximal-operant principle to motivate children's intrinsic interest." Journal of Personality and Social Psychology, 53, 866–879.

Bransford, J.D., & Vye, N.J. (1989). "A perspective on cognitive research and its implications for instruction." In L.B. Resnick and L.E. Klopfer (Eds.), Towards the thinking curriculum: Current cognitive research. 1989 ASCD Yearbook. Alexandria, VA: Association for Supervision and Curriculum Development.

Bridges, E.M. (1984). Managing the incompetent teacher. Eugene, OR: ERIC Clearinghouse on School Management, University of Oregon.

Brookover, W.B., Beamer, L., Efthim, H., Hathaway, D., Lezotte, L., Miller, S., Passalacqua, J., & Tarnatzky, L. (1982). Creating effective schools: An in-service program for enhancing school learning climate and achievement. Holmes Beach, FL: Learning Publications, Inc.

Brophy, J. (1986). On motivating students. East Lansing, MI: Michigan State University.

Brophy, J. (1987). "Synthesis of research on strategies for motivating students to learn." Educational Leadership, 40–48.

Brown, J.S., Collins, A., & Duguid, P. (1989). "Situated cognition and the culture of learning." Educational Research, 18, 32–42.

Brown, A.L., & Campione, J.C. (1992). "Students as researchers and teachers." In J.W. Keefe and H.J. Walberg (Eds.), Teaching for thinking. Reston, VA: National Association of Secondary School Principals.

Buffie, E.G., & Jenkins, J.M. (1971). Curriculum development in nongraded schools. Bloomington, Indiana: Indiana University Press.

Burns, R.W. (1974). Interaction: Place your efforts where the action is." Educational Technology, November, 19–21.

∎C∎

Cizek, G.J. (November, 1995). "The big picture of assessment and who ought to have it." Phi Delta Kappan, 77(3), 246–249.

Cohen, P. (Winter, 1995). "Challenging history: The past remains a battleground for schools." ASCD Curriculum Update.

Collins, A., Brown, J.S., & Newman, S.E. (1989). "Cognitive apprenticeship: Teaching the craft of reading, writing and mathematics." In L.B. Resnick (Ed.), Knowing, learning and instruction: Essays in honor of Robert Glaser. Hillsdale, NJ: Lawrence Erlbaum.

Cooper, J.M. (1991). "Supervision models." In J.W. Keefe and J.M. Jenkins (Eds.). The Instructional Leadership Handbook. Reston, VA: National Association of Secondary School Principals.

Corey, S.M. (1953). Action research to improve school practices. New York: Teachers College.

Corey, S.M. (January, 1944). "The poor scholar's soliloquy." Childhood Education, 20, 219–220.

Csikszentmihalyi, M. (1978). "Intrinsic rewards and emergent motivation." In M.R. Lepper and D. Greene, (Eds.), The hidden costs of rewards: New perspectives on the psychology of human motivation. Hillsdale, NJ: Lawrence Erlbaum.

Csikszentmihalyi, M. (1990). Flow: The psychology of optimal experience. New York: Harper & Row.

∎D∎

Danner, F.W. & Lonky, E. (1981). "A cognitive-developmental approach to the effects of rewards on intrinsic motivation." Child Development, 52, 1043–52.

Day, M., Eisner, E., Stake, R., Wilson, B., & Wilson, M. (1984). Art history, art criticism, and art production: An examination of art education in selected school districts. Chicago: The Rand Corporation.

Deci, E.L. (1978). "Applications of research on the effects of rewards." In M.R. Lepper and D. Greene, (Eds.), The hidden costs of rewards: New perspectives on the psychology of human motivation. Hillsdale, NJ: Lawrence Erlbaum.

Deci, E.L., Spiegel, N.H., Ryan, R.M., Koestner, R., & Kauffman, M. (1982). "Effects of performance standards on teaching styles: Behavior of controlling teachers." Journal of Educational Psychology, 74, 852–859.

Dempsey, R.A., & Traverso, H.P. (1983). Scheduling the secondary school. Reston, VA: National Association of Secondary School Principals.

Dewey, J. (1988/1929). "The quest for certainty." In J.A. Boydston (Ed.), John Dewey: The later works, 1925–1953, Vol. 14. Carbondale, IL: Southern Illinois University Press.

Dow, John A. (1973). "Alternative futures for education and learning: A project for the future." Publication No. OP-106. Philadelphia: Research for Better Schools.

Doyle, W. (1986). "Classroom organization and management." In M.C. Wittrock (Ed.), Handbook of research on teaching, Third edition. New York: Macmillan.

Drucker, Peter (1968). The age of discontinuity. New York: Harper & Row, p. 347.

Dulli, R.E., & Goodman, J.M., (1994). "Geography in a changing world: Reform and renewal." NASSP Bulletin, 78(564), 19–24.

Dweck, C., & Elliott, E., (1983). "Achievement motivation." In P. Mussen (Ed.), Handbook of child psychology. New York: Wiley.

▪E, F▪

Edwards, C.M., Jr., (May, 1995). "Virginia's 4 x 4 high schools: High school, college and more." NASSP Bulletin, 79(571), 23–41.

English, F.W. (1992). Deciding what to teach and test. Newbury Park, CA: Corwin Press.

Farnham-Diggory, S. (1992). Cognitive processes in education, Second Edition. New York: Harper Collins.

Farnham-Diggory, S. (1994). "Paradigms of knowledge and instruction." Review of Educational Research, 64(3), 463–477.

Flake, C.L., Kuhs, T., Donnelly, A., & Ebert, C. (January, 1995). "Reinventing the role of teacher: Teacher as researcher," Phi Delta Kappan, 76(5), 405–407.

Flanders, N.A. (1970). Analyzing teacher behavior. Reading, MA: Addison-Wesley.

Florida Department of Education (1992). Report of the Committee on Educational Assessment. Tallahassee, FL: (unpublished).

Fraser, B.J., & Tobin, K. (1992). "Combining qualitative and quantitative methods in the study of learning environments." In H.C. Waxman and C.D. Ellett (Eds.), The study of learning environments, Vol. 5. Houston, TX: University of Houston.

∎G∎

Gardner, R., Holzman, P.S., Klein, G.S., Tinton, H., & Spence, D.P. (1959). "Cognitive control: A study of individual consistencies in cognitive behavior." Psychological Issues I(4), Monograph 4.

Gardner, H. (1983). Frames of mind: The theory of multiple intelligences. New York: Basic Books.

Gardner, H. (1985). The mind's new science. New York: Basic Books.

Glasser, R., & Nitko, A.J. (1971). "Measurement in learning and instruction. In R.L. Thorndike (Ed.), Educational measurement, Second edition. Washington, DC: American Council on Education.

Glasser, W. (1969). Schools without failure. New York: Harper & Row.

Glasser, W. (1986). Control theory in the classroom. New York: Harper & Row.

Glasser, W. (1994). Control theory manager. New York: Harper Collins Publishers.

Glickman, C.D. (Ed.). (1992). Supervision in transition. 1992 ASCD Yearbook. Alexandria, VA: ASCD.

Good, T.L. (1979). "Teacher effectiveness in the elementary school." Journal of Teacher Education, 30, 52–64.

∎H, I∎

Herman, J.L., Aschbacher, P.R., & Winters, L. (1992). A practical guide to alternative assessment. Alexandria, VA: Association for Supervision and Curriculum Development.

Hopkins, D. (1985). A teacher's guide to classroom research. Philadelphia, PA: Open University Press.

Hubbard, R.S., & Power, B.M. (1992). The art of classroom inquiry. Portsmouth, NH: Heinemann.

Inhelder, B., & Piaget, J. (1958). The growth of logical thinking from childhood to adolescence. New York: Basic Books.

∎J∎

Jackson, P.W. (1968). Life in classrooms. New York: Teachers College Press.

Jenkins, J.M., Letteri, C.A., & Rosenlund, P. (1990). Learning Style Profile handbook, Vol. I: Developing Cognitive skills. Reston, VA: National Association of Secondary School Principals.

Jenkins, J.M. (October, 1994). "Action research: School improvement at the grass roots," International Journal of Educational Reform. 3(4), 470–473.

Jenkins, J.M. (1996). Transforming high schools: A constructivist agenda. Lancaster, PA: Technomic Publishing.

Johnson, D.W., & Johnson, R.T. (1986). Circles of learning: Cooperation in the classroom. Edina, MN: Interaction Book Co.

Joyce, B., & Showers, B. (1982). "The coaching of teaching." Educational Leadership 40, 1:4–10.

Joyce, B., & Weil, B. (1972). Models of teaching. Englewood Cliffs, NJ: Prentice-Hall.

▪K▪

Keefe, J.W. (Ed.) (1979). Student learning styles—Diagnosing and prescribing programs. Reston, VA: National Association of Secondary School Principals.

Keefe, J.W. (Ed.). (1988). Profiling and utilizing learning style. Reston, VA: National Association of Secondary School Principals.

Keefe, J.W. (1989). Learning Style Profile handbook, Vol. II: Accommodating perceptual, study and instructional preferences. Reston, VA: NASSP.

Keefe, J.W. (1989). "Personalized education." In H.J. Walberg and J.L. Lane (Eds.), Organizing for learning: Toward the 21st century. Reston, VA: National Association of Secondary School Principals.

Keefe, J.W. (1991). Learning style: Cognitive and thinking skills. Instructional leadership series. Reston, VA: National Association of Secondary School Principals.

Keefe, J. W. (1993). "Redesigning your school." The High School Magazine, 1(2), 4–9.

Keefe, J.W., & Languis, M.L. (1983). "Operational definitions." Paper presented to the NASSP Learning Styles Task Force, Reston, VA.

Keefe, J.W., & Jenkins, J.M. (1984, 1991). Instructional leadership handbook. Reston, VA: National Association of Secondary School Principals.

Keefe, J.W., Kelley, E.A., & Miller, S.K. (1985). "School climate: Clear definitions and a model for a larger setting." NASSP Bulletin, 69 (484), 70–77.

Keefe, J.W., & Monk, J.S. (1988). Learning Style Profile technical manual. Reston, VA: National Association of Secondary School Principals.

Keefe, J.W., Schmitt, N., Kelley, E.A., & Miller, S.K. (1993). "A comprehensive system for school planning and improvement." In H.J. Walberg, Advances in education productivity, Vol. 3. Greenwich, CT: JAI Press, 257–284.

Keefe, J.W., & Howard, E. (In press). Redesigning schools for the new century: A systems approach. Reston, VA: National Association of Secondary School Principals.

Kintsch, W., & Keenan, J. (1973). "Reading rate and retention as a function of the number of propositions in the base structure of the sentence." Cognitive Psychology, 5, 257–274.

Klein, G.S. (1958). "Cognitive control and motivation." In G. Lindsey (Ed.), Assessment of human motives. New York: Rinehard, 87–118.

Knapp, M.S., Shields, P.M., & Turnbull, B.J. (1992). Academic challenge for the children of poverty: Summary report. Washington, DC: Office of Policy and Planning, U.S. Department of Education.

Knight, S.L., & Waxman, H.C. (1991). "Student's cognition and classroom instruction." In H.C. Waxman and H.J. Walberg (Eds.), Effective teaching: Current research. Berkeley, CA: McCutchen Publishing.

Kohn, A. (1993). Punished by rewards: The trouble with gold stars, incentive plans, A's, praise and other bribes. Boston: Houghton Mifflin Company.

Kruse, C.A., & Kruse, G.D. (May, 1995). "The Master schedule and learning: Improving the quality of education." NASSP Bulletin, 79(571), 1–8.

Kruse, S.D., & Seashore Louis, K. (1995). "An emerging framework for analyzing school-based professional community." Presentation to Center on Organization and Restructuring of Schools, National Advisory Panel, University of Wisconsin-Madison.

∎L∎

Lee, V.E., Groninger, R.G., & Smith, J.B. (1995). "Some summary findings about school organization and restructuring of high schools: Evidence from NELS:88 data." Presentation to Center on Organization and Restructuring of Schools, National Advisory Panel, University of Wisconsin-Madison.

Leonhardt, M. (1993). Parents who love reading, kids who don't. New York: Crown Publishers.

Lepper, M.R. (1988). "Motivational considerations in the study of instruction. Cognition and Instruction 5, 289–230.

Lepper, M.R., & Cordova, D.I. (1975). "A desire to be taught: Instructional consequences and intrinsic motivation." Motivation and Emotion, 16:187–208.

Lepper, M.R., & Greene, D. (1978). The hidden costs of reward: New perspectives on the psychology of human motivation. Hillsdale, NJ: Lawrence Erlbaum.

Lesgold, A. (1988). "Problem solving." In R.J. Sternberg and E.E. Smith (Eds.), The psychology of human thought. New York: Cambridge University Press.

Letteri, C.A. (1976). Cognitive style: "Implications for curriculum." In A. Molnar and J. Zaharik (Eds.), Curriculum theory. Washington, DC: Association for Supervision and Curriculum Development.

Letteri, C.A. (1985). "Teaching students how to learn." Theory Into Practice, XXIV(2), 112–122.

Letteri, C.A. (1988). "The NASSP Learning Style Profile and cognitive processing." In J.W. Keefe (Ed.), Profiling and utilizing learning style. Reston, VA: National Association of Secondary School Principals.

Lewin, K. (1948). Resolving social conflicts. New York: Harper and Brothers.

■M■

Marzano, R., Pickering, D., & McTighe, J. (1993). Assessing student outcomes: Performance assessment using the dimension of learning model. Alexandra, VA: Association for Supervision and Curriculum Development.

Maslow, A.H. (1970). Motivation and personality. New York: Harper & Row.

Messick, S., & Associates. (1976). Individuality in learning. San Francisco: Jossey-Bass.

Moos, R.M. (1974). The school climate scales: An overview. Palo Alto, CA: Consulting Psychologists Press.

National Association of Secondary School Principals, (1996), Breaking ranks: Changing an American institution. Reston, VA,: National Association of Secondary School Principals.

National Center for Education Statistics. (1993). The condition of education. Washington, DC: U.S. Government Printing Office.

National Research Council. (1989). Everybody counts: A report to the nation on the future of mathematics education. Washington, DC: National Academy Press.

Nevis, E.C., Di Bella, A.J., & Gould, J.M. (Winter, 1993). "Understanding organizations as learning systems." Sloan Management Review, 36, 85–92.

Newmann, F.M., Ed. (1995). School restructing and student learning, Prospectus. Madison, WI: Center on Organization and Restructuring of Schools, University of Wisconsin.

Newmann, F.M., Marks, H.M., & Gamoran, A. (1995). "Authentic pedagogy and student performance." Paper presented to the annual meeting of the American Educational Research Association, San Francisco, CA.

Newmann, F.M., Secada, W.G., & Wehlage, G.G. (1995). A guide to authentic instruction and assessment: Vision, standards and scoring. Madison: Wisconsin Center for Education Research, University of Wisconsin.

Newmann, F.M., & Wehlage, G.G. (1995). Successful school restructuring. Madison, WI: Wisconsin Center for Education Research, University of Wisconsin.

■O, P■

O'Neil, J. (1995). "On schools as learning organizations: A conversation with Peter Senge." Educational Leadership, 52(7), 20–23.

Ornstein, A.C. (1991). "Teacher effectiveness research: Theoretical considerations." In H.C. Waxman and H.J. Walberg. Current teaching: Current research. Berkeley, CA: McCutchen.

Page, E.B., & Petersen, N.S., (1995). "The computer moves into essay grading: Updating the ancient test." Phi Delta Kappan, 76(7), 561–565.

Palincsar, A.S., & Brown, A.L. (1984). Reciprocal teaching of comprehension-fostering and comprehension-monitoring activities." Cognition and Instruction, 2, 117–175.

Pearson, D. (1985). "Reading comprehension instruction: Six necessary steps." Reading Teacher, 38, 724–738.

Pellicer, L.O., Anderson, L.W., Keefe, J.W., Kelley, E.A., & McCleary, L.E. (1990). High school leaders and their schools, Vol. II: Profiles of effectiveness. Reston, VA: National Association of Secondary School Principals.

Peterson, G.A. (1994). "Geography and technology in the classroom." NASSP Bulletin. 78(564), 25–29.

Phillips, D.C. (1995). "The good, the bad, and the ugly: The many faces of constructivism." Educational Researcher, 24(7), 5–12.

Phye, G.D., & Andre, T. (Eds.) (1986). Cognitive classroom learning: Understanding, thinking and problem solving. Orlando: Academic Press.

Poole, W.L. (1994). "Removing the super from supervisor." Journal of Curriculum and Supervision, 9(3), 284–309.

Posner, G.J., Strike, K.A., Hewson, P.W., & Gertzog, W.A. (1982). "Accommodation of scientific conception: Toward a theory of conceptual change." Science Education, 66, 211–227.

Prawat, R.S. (1995). "Misreading Dewey: Reform projects and the language game." Educational Researcher, 24(7), 13–22.

▪R▪

Ramsey, W., & Ransley, W. (1986). "A method of analysis for determining dimensions of teaching style." Teaching and Teacher Education, 2, 69–79.

Raphael, J., & Greenberg, R. (October, 1995). "Image processing: A state of the art way to learn science." Educational Leadership, 53–2.

Regional Educational Laboratory Network, B. Williams (Ed.) (1995). Closing the urban achievement gap: A vision to guide change in beliefs and practice. Philadelphia: Research for Better Schools.

Resnick, L.B., & Klopfer, L.E. (1989). "Toward the thinking curriculum: An overview." In L.B. Resnick (Ed.), Knowing, learning and instruction: Essays in honor of Robert Glaser. Hillsdale, NJ: Lawrence Erlbaum.

Resnick, L.B., & Resnick, D.P. (1989). "Tests as standards of achievement in school." In Proceedings of the 1989 ETS invitational conference: The uses of standardized tests in American education. Princeton, NJ: Educational Testing Service.

Rosenshine, B., & Guenther, J. (1992). "Using scaffolds for teaching higher level cognitive strategies." In J.W. Keefe & H.J. Walberg (Eds.), Teaching for thinking. Reston, VA: National Association of Secondary School Principals.

Rosenshine, B., & Stevens, R. (1986). "Teaching functions." In M.C. Wittrock (Ed.), Handbook of research on teaching, Third edition. New York: Macmillan.

Rowe, M.B. (1974). "Relation of wait-time and rewards to the development of language, logic, and fate control: Part II—Rewards." Journal of Research in Science Teaching, 11, 291–308.

Ryan, J.M., & Miyasaka, J.R. (1995). "Current practices in testing and assessment: What is driving the changes?" NASSP Bulletin, 70(573), 1–10.

∎S∎

Sautter, R.C. (February, 1994). "An arts education school reform strategy." Phi Delta Kappan, 75(6), 432–437.

Schoenfeld, A.H. (1985). Mathematical problem solving. New York: Academic Press.

Schon, D.A. (1988). "Coaching reflective teaching." In P.O. Grimmett and G.L. Erickson (Eds.). Reflection in teacher education. New York: Teachers College Press.

Schultz, R.A. (1982). "Teaching style and sociopsychological climates." Alberta Journal of Educational Research, 28, 9–18.

Senge, P.M. (1990). The fifth discipline: The art and practice of the learning organization. New York: Doubleday/Currency.

Senge, P.M., Roberts, C., Ross, R.B., Smith, B.J., & Kleiner, A. (1994). The fifth discipline fieldbook. New York: Currency/Doubleday.

Sergiovanni, T.J. (1990). Value-added leadership: How to get extraordinary performance in schools. New York: Harcourt Brace Jovanovich.

Sizer, T.R. (1992). Horace's school: Redesigning the american high school. Boston: Houghton Mifflin Company.

Slavin, R.E. (1993). Cooperative Learning. New York: Longman.

Slavin, R.E. (1991). "Synthesis of research on cooperative learning." Educational Leadership, 48(5), 71–82.

Smith, M.L. (1993). The role of high-stakes testing in school reform. Washington, DC: National Education Association.

Soar, R.S., & Soar, R.M. (1983). "Context effects in the teaching-learning process." In D.C. Smith (Ed.), Essential knowledge for beginning educators. Washington, DC: American Association of Colleges for Teacher Education.

Sternberg, R.J. (1982). "Intelligence as thinking and learning skills." Human Intelligence, Jan/Feb.

Sternberg, R.J. (Ed.) (1985). Human abilities: An information-processing approach. New York: W.H. Freeman and Co.

Stiggins, R.J. (1995). Student centered classroom assessment. New York: Macmillan.

Stiggins, R.J. (1995). "Assessment literacy for the 21st century," Phi Delta Kappan, 77(3), 238–245.

Stolp, S., & Smith, S.C. (1995). Transforming school culture: Stories, symbols, values and the leader's role. Eugene, OR: ERIC Clearinghouse on Educational Management.

∎T∎

Taylor, E., & Frye, B. (1988). Skills pretest: Replacing unnecessary skill activities with pleasure reading comprehension strategy instruction." Unpublished manuscript. College of Education, University of Minnesota.

Thomson, S.D. (Ed.). (1993). Principals for our changing schools. Fairfax, VA: National Policy Board for Educational Administration.

Thorndike, E.L. (1918). "The nature, purposes, and general methods of measurements of educational products." In The measure of educational products, Seventeenth Yearbook of the National Society for the Study of Education, Part II. Bloomington, IN: Public School Publishing Co.

Thurstone, L.L. (1944). A factorial study of perception. Psychometric Monograph No. 4. Chicago: University of Chicago.

Tobin, K., & Fraser, B.J. (1991). "Learning from exemplary teachers." In H.C. Waxman and H.J. Walberg (Eds.), Effective teaching: Current research. Berkeley, CA: McCutchen Publishing.

Travers, R.M.W. (1982). Essentials of learning—The new cognitive learning for students of education, Fifth edition. New York: Macmillan.

Tulving, E. (1972). "Episodic and semantic memory." In E. Tulving and W. Donaldson (Eds.), Organization and memory. New York: Academic Press.

∎V, W, Z∎

Vygotsky, L.S. (1962). Thought and language. (E. Haufmann and G. Vakar, Eds. & Trans.). Cambridge, MA: MIT Press.

Vygotsky, L.S. (1978). Mind in society. Cambridge, MA: Harvard University Press.

Walberg, H.J. (1984). "Improving the productivity of America's schools." Educational Leadership, 41, 19–27.

Walberg, H.J. (1990). "Productive teaching and instruction: Assessing the knowledge base." Phi Delta Kappan, February, 470–478.

Watkins, M.J. (1974). "Concept and measurements of primary memory." Psychological Bulletin, 81, 695–711.

Waxman, H.C., & Ellett, C.D. (Eds.) (1992). The study of learning environments, Vol. 5. Houston, TX: University of Houston.

Wiggins, G. (1993). Assessing student performances. San Francisco, CA: Jossey-Bass, Inc.

Wong, M.R., & Raulerson, J.D. (1974). A guide to systematic instructional design. Englewood Cliffs, NJ: Educational Technology Publications.

Zepeda, S. (1995). The supervisory continuum: A developmental approach," The Practitioner, 22(1), 1–4.